About This Book

Why is this topic important?

When organizations without formal training departments need training, they often find themselves in the position of creating "accidental trainers" out of their human resource generalists, subject matter experts, and managers. It's a great idea and the perfect start of the evolution of a more formal training department. Unfortunately these accidental trainers can find themselves overwhelmed as they try to learn their new role without mentors and models.

What can you achieve with this book?

The Accidental Trainer addresses managing each of the roles and responsibilities of an accidental trainer, from budgeting to booking rooms for training or coaxing a fellow worker into becoming a de facto trainer. The intention is to help readers to efficiently accomplish the most that they can while working within the constraints of being a small, part-time, or one-person training department.

How is this book organized?

The book is divided into nine chapters and three major themes. The first four chapters deal with common "baseline" activities such as understanding the roles and responsibilities of an accidental trainer, establishing an identity within the organization, developing vital relationships and alliances both inside the company and within the business community, understanding how to budget or fund training offerings, and providing practical advice for organization and project management. Chapter Four includes an extensive section on free or low-cost technology resources that allow a small or one-person training department to be more effective and efficient.

Chapters Five through Eight offer practical strategies for creating and rolling out various types of training offerings—from designing and conducting a homegrown training workshop to hiring vendors and outsourcing training deliverables. Chapter Seven, in particular, offers a wealth of ideas for delivering training to your employees without doing so yourself. Finally, Chapter Nine offers ideas for taking your role and new training department to the next level of capabilities.

About Pfeiffer

Pfeiffer serves the professional development and hands-on resource needs of training and human resource practitioners and gives them products to do their jobs better. We deliver proven ideas and solutions from experts in HR development and HR management, and we offer effective and customizable tools to improve workplace performance. From novice to seasoned professional, Pfeiffer is the source you can trust to make yourself and your organization more successful.

Essential Knowledge Pfeiffer produces insightful, practical, and comprehensive materials on topics that matter the most to training and HR professionals. Our Essential Knowledge resources translate the expertise of seasoned professionals into practical, how-to guidance on critical workplace issues and problems. These resources are supported by case studies, worksheets, and job aids and are frequently supplemented with CD-ROMs, websites, and other means of making the content easier to read, understand, and use.

Essential Tools Pfeiffer's Essential Tools resources save time and expense by offering proven, ready-to-use materials—including exercises, activities, games, instruments, and assessments—for use during a training or team-learning event. These resources are frequently offered in looseleaf or CD-ROM format to facilitate copying and customization of the material.

Pfeiffer also recognizes the remarkable power of new technologies in expanding the reach and effectiveness of training. While e-hype has often created whizbang solutions in search of a problem, we are dedicated to bringing convenience and enhancements to proven training solutions. All our e-tools comply with rigorous functionality standards. The most appropriate technology wrapped around essential content yields the perfect solution for today's on-the-go trainers and human resource professionals.

Essential resources for training and HR professionals

THE ACCIDENTAL TRAINER

THE ACCIDENTAL TRAINER

A Reference Manual for the Small, Part-Time, or One-Person Training Department

Nanette Miner, Ed.D.

Pfeiffer
A Wiley Imprint
www.pfeiffer.com

Published by Pfeiffer
An Imprint of Wiley
989 Market Street, San Francisco, CA 94103-1741
www.pfeiffer.com

For additional copies/bulk purchases of this book in the U.S. please contact 800-274-4434.

Pfeiffer books and products are available through most bookstores. To contact Pfeiffer directly call our Customer Care Department within the U.S. at 800-274-4434, outside the U.S. at 317-572-3985, fax 317-572-4002, or visit www.pfeiffer.com.

Pfeiffer also publishes its books in a variety of electronic formats. Some content that appears in print may not be available in electronic books.

Library of Congress Cataloging-in-Publication Data

Miner, Nanette, date.
    The accidental trainer: a reference manual for the small, part-time, or one-person training department/Nanette Miner.
        p. cm.
    Includes bibliographical references and index.
    ISBN-13: 978–0–7879–8046–7 (pbk.)
    ISBN-10: 0–7879–8046–3 (pbk.)
1. Employees—Training of. 2. Employee training personnel. I. Title.
    HF5549.5.T7M556 2006
    658.3'124—dc22

                                        2006006228

Acquiring Editor: Lisa Shannon

Director of Development: Kathleen Dolan Davies

Developmental Editor: Susan Rachmeler

Production Editor: Rachel Anderson

Editor: Beverly Miller

Manufacturing Supervisor: Becky Carreño

Editorial Assistant: Jesse Wiley

Illustrations: Lotus Art

Printed in the United States of America

Printing   10   9   8   7   6   5   4   3   2   1

Contents

Acknowledgments

I AM GRATEFUL to a number of people who helped to shape and refine this book:

All of my wonderful clients who have each taught me something new and practical and who inspired me to say, "More people need to know about this!"

My professional colleagues who proofread and copyedited the first drafts of chapters and made useful comments such as, "I have no idea what you're trying to say!": Jennifer Hofmann, Dr. Sharon Abrahams, Gary Steinkohl, Anita Taylor, and Julie Hartland.

Researcher extraordinaire Rachel Hyland, who actually likes looking for the needle in the haystack and returns value in addition to data.

And finally, many, many thanks to my developmental editor, Jeffrey Leeson, who made the most extraordinary suggestions and could see the forest through the trees, when I couldn't.

Introduction

WELCOME TO ONE of the most exciting professional fields: workplace training. Many of us, including me, did not choose training as our first career; we came to training "accidentally." Training can be one of the most stimulating professions available because of the variety of tasks and responsibilities involved and because each day we get to see the positive impact of our work—in the workplace in general, and more specifically on people's faces. I predict that you will enjoy your role as a trainer immensely.

You may feel all alone at the moment, but in fact, you are in good company. According to the American Society for Training and Development, there are more informal training organizations than there are formal training departments within U.S. businesses. When organizations without formal training departments need to provide training, they often find themselves in the position of creating "accidental trainers" out of their human resource generalists, subject matter experts, and managers. It's a great idea and the perfect start in the evolution of a more formal training department. Unfortunately these accidental trainers can find themselves overwhelmed as they try to learn their new role without mentors and models. Most businesses do not commit to a formal training department until they have at least three hundred employees; more often, you won't find a training department until a company has grown to about two thousand employees. And yet training is still accomplished each day through people just like you: accidental trainers.

Accidental trainers come from varied backgrounds, yet they all share one common characteristic: they have been thrust into the role of training. Maybe you recognize yourself among this group of accidental trainers:

- A human resource generalist who squeezes training in and among his other duties such as recruiting, hiring, compensation, and benefits administration.

- A subject matter expert who has been tapped by management because she is the best in this position. It is a common misconception that because someone is good at what she does she can train others to do it.

- A department manager or small business owner. In small and mid-sized companies, training often becomes the responsibility of a department manager or the business owner.

- An individual who has been tapped to begin a training department where one hasn't existed before.

As we learn any new skill, we tend to do things the hard way. Without an experienced mentor to assist us, we frequently waste time and money making avoidable mistakes. *The Accidental Trainer* is intended to help you, no matter which definition best describes your situation, to understand your role and responsibilities and guide you in making the right choices for increasing the capabilities of your organization, through training. I welcome you to the profession and hope that you come to love it as I do.

What *The Accidental Trainer* Will Do for You

My intention for this book is to help prevent you from reinventing the wheel by giving you the information you need, when you need it, as well as assisting you in doing your job better, faster, and cheaper. I have endeavored to compile what might take a new trainer five or more years to learn through trial and error into one reference that can be used on a need-to-know basis. The book covers various how-to's as well as providing suggestions for efficiently handling the day-to-day administration of a training "department." I don't expect that you will read the book from beginning to end, but rather that you will use it as a resource to find the answers you need when you need them.

Since you, the readers of this book, have varied roles and responsibilities, the examples and suggestions provided here are generic enough that you should be able to take the tactical concept and transform it so that it is practical for your own organization. In addition, I have provided worksheets that you can modify for your own use to keep track of your many responsibilities and efficiently accomplish your goals.

How This Book Came About

I have worked as a training consultant for over fifteen years, and many of my clients are accidental trainers. What I have noticed is how much each individual struggles to come up with the right answers to training objectives. It pains me to see folks reinventing the wheel because they don't know what questions to ask or where to look for an answer. I have been very happy to help lighten the load, but after a decade of assisting, it dawned on me that it would be a very long process to try to reach every accidental trainer on a one-to-one basis. A second inspiration for *The Accidental Trainer* is the many tricks that my clients have taught *me*. For instance I have learned about free Web-based surveying tools, creating a "brand" for the training department, and how to influence other individuals within the organization to become de facto trainers. Each time another great idea came my way, I was frustrated with my inability to share it with every other accidental trainer who was struggling with the same issues; I wanted to create a resource that all accidental trainers could use to get the answers they need.

What the Book Does and Does Not Cover

The Accidental Trainer addresses managing each of your roles and responsibilities: helping you to efficiently accomplish the most that you can while working within the constraints of being a small, part-time, or one-person training department. I have sought to create a resource that does not duplicate information presented in other books. For instance, this book does not teach presentation skills or ponder whether e-learning is a better approach for your material than a classroom-based training course. The answers to these common training challenges are readily available from other excellent, and more expert, resources, and when appropriate, I suggest them throughout the text.

How *The Accidental Trainer* Is Organized

Chapters One through Three provide a basic grounding in the new role you've taken on, including many of the responsibilities and challenges you will face. These chapters will help you understand your role in the organization, as well as how you might maximize your effectiveness by building relationships and addressing training needs.

Chapter Four is full of suggestions and practical strategies for time management, project management, and general organizational skills required of an accidental trainer. Using the techniques and worksheets set out in this chapter should help you to feel less overwhelmed by the many tasks that are required to create and implement training programs. In addition, a number of useful technology-based tools are reviewed, which will help you to fulfill your role more efficiently.

Chapter Five focuses on the task that you will undoubtedly fulfill most often: producing training programs. It explains various types of training events and how to plan for and carry them out and includes a helpful worksheet that will enable you to execute the administrative side of a classroom-based training program.

Chapters Six and Seven enable you to maximize your efficiency by using a number of resources wisely. In addition to outsourcing many tasks, as discussed in Chapter Six on how to choose and work with vendors, you may also be able to use a number of free or low-cost training resources that are available to you locally, the topic of Chapter Seven. These two chapters focus on helping you to use your time wisely and to accomplish more than a one-person or part-time training department could be expected to accomplish, making you a hero within your organization.

Chapter Eight provides a broad overview of concepts and tasks that should be attended to when you find that you need to create a customized training offering yourself. From conducting a needs analysis to developing training materials, this chapter offers many how-to's and worksheets for speeding the process and producing accurate results.

Finally, Chapter Nine presents a few ideas for your next steps, growing your training department, and taking your own skills and abilities to the next level of success.

Terms that may not be familiar to you are explained the first time they appear. Boxes provide examples or illustrations designed to assist you with concepts I've introduced, and checklists or worksheets are provided so that many of your tasks can be narrowed down to "fill in the blank" activities.

How to Get the Most from This Resource

You do not have to read *The Accidental Trainer* from start to finish. The chapters are not dependent on one another. Each contains its own body of information from which you can learn and fully put into practice. For example, if one of your first needs is to locate and begin to work with a training vendor, turn to Chapter Seven to learn the best way to go about it. When a concept is discussed that references information that would be helpful to know and appears in another chapter, that chapter is cited so that you can easily locate the supporting information.

The Additional Resources section at the end of the book lists many resources that will help you to solve virtually any challenge you may face, such as finding software, public seminar companies, or professional associations. Because *The Accidental Trainer* represents what is available as of its date of publication, I will continue to add new resources to this book's companion Web site, www.TheAccidentalTrainer.com. Note that all of the checklists and worksheets in this book are also available at the Web site, so that you can download them and customize them to fit your own organization's needs.

You may wish to sign up for the monthly "TAT News," which is broadcast by e-mail the first Friday of every month and offers tips for all aspects of an accidental trainer's responsibilities. "TAT News" is also a community of practice for accidental trainers, allowing you to pose questions or challenges to fellow accidental trainers and get responses from others who are doing the same type of work and facing the same daily challenges as you. You can also sign up for the monthly newsletter from www.TheAccidentalTrainer.com.

Disclaimer

The Accidental Trainer references a number of resources, including Web sites; this requires a word of caution because Web site addresses change, companies merge and change hands, and products disappear. My mention of a particular product or resource should not be construed to mean that similar offerings are not good; rather, I have based my recommendations on four criteria:

- It is a product or service that I have used myself.

- It is an economical solution.

- It is simple, self-explanatory, or painless to use.

- It is professional in its appearance or execution.

If you know of other resources that would make a fellow accidental trainer's life easier, please submit them at www.TheAccidentalTrainer.com, and together we can get the word out.

Summary

Remember that you don't need to read this book in order. You can dive right in at any topic for which you need help today. If you'd like a general overview of your new position, Chapter One introduces you to the responsibilities as well as the rewards and challenges you'll encounter. You may be trying to manage some of these concepts right now. Good luck, and remember, *The Accidental Trainer* is here for you when you need a helping hand.

THE ACCIDENTAL TRAINER

The Rewards, Challenges, and Responsibilities of an Accidental Trainer

A S THE SOLE INDIVIDUAL responsible for training in your organization or department, you'll be seen as the "go-to" person in a number of instances. When a departmental manager believes he or she has a training problem, you'll be the first person contacted. Upper management will look to you to help them make decisions about how to increase productivity and the skill level of the workforce. The human resource department may look to you to help with new hire training or to conduct training on effective performance reviews. One of the exciting aspects about being an accidental trainer is that your role constantly changes—not only on a daily basis but sometimes even on an hourly basis. In this chapter, we'll discuss the rewards and challenges of your new position as expressed by experienced accidental trainers and take a look at the many roles and responsibilities you can look forward to fulfilling. In short, the chapter will let you know what to expect and start to prepare you to excel in your dynamic new position.

Rewards and Challenges

Being an accidental trainer can be both exhausting and exhilarating. On one hand, you have limited time and resources available to you, which can be an ongoing and wearying struggle. On the other hand, these challenges force you to develop creative solutions that are applicable to your company's unique situations. At the end of each day, you'll be able to look back and say, "Wow! Look what I accomplished today!" Because I am in contact with so many accidental trainers on a regular basis, I conducted an informal poll, asking them to tell me about the rewards and challenges of their position. To share their experienced perspective with you, I've compiled their responses.

Rewards of the Role

The primary purpose of training is to move the organization as a whole to greater achievements. There is quite a bit of satisfaction in knowing that you have contributed significantly to the strategic goals of your company. Something as simple as new hire training can result in bottom-line savings of thousands of dollars. How? This training can result in reduced turnover in the first ninety days of employment, it can assist an individual in becoming a productive member of the workforce more quickly, and it can help to introduce individuals to the culture of the organization, which can help them more easily assimilate into your company. In addition, one of the rewards of being a trainer is seeing individuals grow professionally and knowing that you helped them achieve their new knowledge and skills.

An often underappreciated reward of being an accidental trainer is autonomy and independence. In many cases, you will naturally be seen as the expert in training, and your opinions and recommendations will be sought. You may find that once the training department has been established, you will be overwhelmed with requests for training and personnel development from various departments within your organization. Because your time and resources will dictate how many projects you can take on, you'll be in the enviable position to pick and choose those projects that will do the most good for the organization or that you will find personally rewarding and challenging.

Finally, one of the finest rewards that will come from being an accidental trainer is the knowledge and skills that you will develop and be able to apply immediately to the performance of your organization. You will inevitably become more skilled at public speaking and group facilitation, skills that all organizations look for in leaders. Your organizational skills will become top-notch thanks to the constant responsibility of project and meeting planning, which will contribute in untold ways to both your professional and personal life. And almost every day, you'll be able to see the immediate impact that your personal contribution brings to your organization. There may not be a more diverse, multifaceted, and potentially satisfying role in the organization for an individual who wants to develop skills while moving individuals and the organization toward excellence.

The Challenges of Your Role

No new role comes without the challenge of learning what that role is about. What are the expectations, who will you interact with, and how will your success be judged? Inevitably you'll learn by doing. Unfortunately the learn-by-doing mode can cause emergencies and unplanned events to arise. One of the goals of *The Accidental Trainer* is to help you think through each responsibility you are taking on, so that you don't find yourself in emergency mode too often.

The volume of work that you will be responsible for will greatly constrict your time for personal development and growth in areas that don't immediately support the initiatives on which you are working. It is important that you make time to learn about the industry and stay current with resources that are available to you; otherwise you'll find yourself living the cliché, "When all you have is a hammer, every problem is a nail." In other words, you'll attempt to apply the same solution to each training problem rather than being able to apply the right solution from a menu of appropriate choices.

This next challenge is not limited to a trainer's role; it is the ever-present challenge of limited resources. In addition to having limited funds and time, you'll find the lack of other human resources to be limiting in many ways: if you want to invite attendees to a training program, *you* will be sending the e-mail invitation; when attendees begin to sign up for the training, *you* will be the registrar; *you* may even be the person in the mailroom at 8:00 P.M. the night before the training, copying and collating the materials; and very often *you* will be the one presenting the training as well.

You'll need to overcome the common idea that training is easy; you may even believe this yourself if you've been in your role for a short time. Creating training that is efficient for the organization (meaning it doesn't waste people's time or organizational resources) and effective and engaging for the participants (meaning it enables them to return to the job with enhanced skills and knowledge) is an art form. Other individuals in your organization who don't have a training role will find it hard to comprehend that it would take forty hours or more to create a two-hour training class because it looks so effortless when they are sitting in the audience. The challenge for you will be to request (nay, demand!) the appropriate time resources in order to do your job effectively.

Finally, accidental trainers can find themselves so overwhelmed with work that they rarely pick their heads up to see what is going on around them. This can lead to discouragement and burnout in the job and to the reputation in the organization that the training department doesn't link with the business itself. One way to be successful in your role is to be proactive about the potential for training rather than simply reactive to requests for training (when fires may already be burning).

The rewards and challenges just described give you a big-picture view of what you can expect. At the end of your first year in your new role, you'll look back on the work you've done and describe it overall just as it has been described here.

The Accidental Trainer's Many Roles

The role that you play may change rapidly. Some roles will be more global, such as a consultant or manager, and others will be more task specific, such as instructional designer or presenter. The global roles are things you and others may not be able to easily identify or define, so addressing them here should give you a better understanding of how a trainer supports the organization as a whole.

Global Roles

A recent study suggested that trainers, especially those who are the sole person responsible for training in their organization, spend at least half their time performing more global support functions of consultant, coach, performance improvement specialist, manager, and technical guru rather than actually training people.

Consultant. Approaching your role from a consultant's perspective may be one of the more difficult tasks you will have to perform. Because the role of a trainer is innately a supportive function, one that exists to assist the rest of the organization to improve its performance, it's sometimes difficult to keep the consultant's perspective, which is one of impartial analysis. When acting as a consultant, you should approach training requests as assignments in which you will thoughtfully consider the needs of the workforce, the goals of the organization, and the best way to achieve an improved performance outcome. You will need to resist the temptation to immediately tackle any request that comes to you and instead approach the request as if you know little about the organization or the department that made the request. Sometimes what appears to be a training need really isn't and requires a different solution—for example, hiring a new employee or purchasing a new piece of equipment. Maintaining a consultant's perspective will enable you to gather information and data to make the right recommendations for the organization. Eventually you'll become adept at asking the right questions, looking for deeper meaning in the answers that you get, and never accepting a situation at face value.

The box sets out the types of questions you may want to ask of a manager who is requesting training. These are addressed more thoroughly in Chapter Eight when we discuss how to analyze whether a training need exists.

Fifteen Consulting Questions to Ask

1. What is the problem you are experiencing?

2. What are the symptoms that led you to believe this was a problem?

3. Who is the audience?

4. Tell me about their typical day.

5. Why do you think this is a training need?

6. What training exists already?

7. What training has the audience had in the past?

8. Have they been able to do the job [or task or skill] in the past?

9. What organizational factors might be playing a role?

10. Does the audience think they need training [now or for this problem]?

11. What if you don't train them? What's the worst that will happen?

12. How will this training need tie to business goals?

13. What resources are you able to contribute to assist with the training?

14. How will you know when the problem has been addressed? What do you want to see changed or done differently?

15. How will you reinforce your workers' new knowledge and skills once they return to the job?

I learned a lesson about asking the right questions during my first consulting assignment—and I did not learn it the easy way. I was asked to provide customer service training for an inside sales group that had been receiving poor reviews from their customer base. I accepted the request at face value and designed an eight-hour customer service training class. We split the group in two, and I worked with half the group one day and half the group the following day.

About two hours into the first session, I had a horrible realization that I was preaching to the choir. This group of trainees was very dedicated to providing excellent customer service and knew all the right things to say and do. In order not to waste their time, I asked them why they believed their customers were complaining about their service. I was told that customers frequently requested faxed copies of their bill of lading or invoices, but this group did not possess its own fax machine (this was back when a fax machine cost well over five hundred dollars), so they were forced to leave their desk and walk down the hall to use the machine in another department. This resulted in poor customer service in two ways: incoming calls and response time. Either the salespeople were frequently away from their desks trying to send a fax and therefore unavailable to take calls, resulting in longer queue times, or they would wait until it seemed to be a good time to leave in an effort to not leave their department short-staffed, which might mean a twenty- or thirty-minute wait before they had the opportunity to walk down the hall to the fax machine.

I could have saved the client a lot of time and money in terms of paying my fee, as well as taking the sales group off the floor for training, if I had simply said, "Tell me about their typical day." Two simple solutions, neither of which required training, would have become apparent: (1) the client could have invested in a fax machine for the inside sales group, or (2) the salespeople could simply have changed their work process by designating one representative to take all the faxes, once per hour, to the fax down the hall and in the interim the salespeople could tell callers, "I'll get that to you as soon as possible; it may take up to ninety minutes." The first option would have been an economical and long-term solution, and the second option would have given customers a better point of reference regarding what "poor service" looked like. If the second option had been adopted and the fax arrived in sixty minutes rather than the expected ninety, their customers would have been delighted with the service they received.

Manager. Being a one-person or part-time training department will require you to be good at self-management; however, a more global perspective of a manager is a "person who leads or directs all or part of an organization, through the deployment and manipulation of resources (human, financial, material, intellectual or intangible)" (www.wikipedia.org). This is an exact definition of your managerial responsibilities. You may not have the title "manager," but management will be a significant daily responsibility as you coordinate people, facilities, materials production, and distribution, competing time lines, and the business goals of the individual departments that you support. In addition you'll be responsible for managing resources such as money (more in Chapter Three), deadlines (more in Chapter Four), and both internal and external human resources.

Coach. Being a coach may be your primary responsibility as an accidental trainer due to the constraints that you will find yourself operating within. One of the most efficient ways to develop other people is through coaching them. A coach helps an individual to define his or her goals and create a plan of action to achieve them. Much like an athletic coach, the workplace coach offers suggestions for improvement, helps the individual to refine his or her technique, and provides ongoing encouragement and support. In other words, the coach does not actually do the work. While you will provide guidance, support, and ongoing encouragement for the individual, the responsibility for acquiring the new skills or knowledge lies squarely with the individual. You may also find yourself coaching a manager so that she in turn is able to improve the performance of her own group. This approach is especially common in smaller companies where there may not be enough people to fill a training class.

New attorneys learn their skills on the job, not in law school. A law firm with sixteen offices throughout the United States implemented a formal coaching relationship for new attorneys. The new attorneys are paired with one or more seasoned attorney coaches in order to develop their skills in areas such as oratory, negotiation, and marketing their services.

Performance Improvement Specialist. A performance improvement specialist is part consultant, part trainer, and part business manager. Like a consultant, performance improvement specialists look at the big picture to identify causes of poor performance and the appropriate ways to address the situation. Although both a performance improvement specialist and a trainer are focused on increasing the performance of the business overall, the distinction lies in the fact that the performance improvement specialist looks at all approaches to solving the problem, not just training-related approaches. A trainer applies processes that address workers' lack of knowledge or skill and affect their ability to do a job correctly; the performance improvement specialist addresses anything within the organization that may resolve poor performance. For instance, perhaps the organization has poor product quality because there are no consequences for workers who do not perform quality control on their work. Performance may be improved in this case by giving rewards or instituting consequences, both nontraining solutions that are effective ways of improving performance.

Technical Guru. Technology enables us to deliver training to participants across the globe, right at their desks. You may find yourself in charge of teleconferences, webinars, computer-based training (more about these in Chapter Eight), or a number of other technology-based delivery methods. Although you won't necessarily have to know how to work the technology, you will need to have a good understanding of what method of delivery would be more appropriate than another in a given situation. You'll also need to know what the technological capabilities of your organization are—both people and equipment. Are employees computer literate? Do they have ready access to a computer? Do the computers have CDs, speakers, and Internet access? I recommend becoming friends with the people in the information technology (IT) department; you'll find you interact with them a lot, and you'll want them to know who you are and understand that your goal is to help the organization, not to slow them down.

Task-Oriented Responsibilities

In contrast to the global roles you will fulfill, which are more or less invisible to an observer, other people in your organization will acknowledge when you are performing a training task. What follows is hardly an all-inclusive list of the various responsibilities, but it is a good grounding in what you can expect to do on a weekly, if not daily, basis. These tasks typically result in an end product or at least a move along a project plan path. You can use these descriptions when people ask, "What do you do?"

Training Designer. Many organizations find that they need to custom-design training for their employees because the work that they do is unique or proprietary. For example, in almost all cases, a new hire training program is custom-designed for an organization because it is unique to the way that the organization does business. One of the reasons that you were appointed an accidental trainer may be that your organization determined it had unique needs that it could not find training for off the shelf.

> **TIP** ▷ Off-the-shelf training is generic training that is designed by a training vendor. You may purchase the rights to deliver the training at your site. Off-the-shelf programs are commonly found for sales, customer service, and software training and may include videos, audiotape, Web-based programs, or leader and participant materials in a complete package for classroom delivery.

The designer of training programs conceptualizes what the training should include. For example, I once developed a two-day course called Shoe U for a retail client. The goal of the course was to teach footwear salespeople the differences in the eight athletic footwear brands the retailer carried along with selling skills such as determining needs and suggesting add-on sales. The training director at the company conceptualized the overall design. Day One was to be all about product knowledge, and Day Two was to be designed as a game in order to balance out the intensity of Day One. With that high-level design, the development work was left to me.

As a training designer, you may interview subject matter experts to determine what knowledge needs to be transmitted to the trainees, you will order the information into a logical presentation sequence, you will consider the best way to deliver each topic within the training, and you will begin to determine how to evaluate trainees' success.

Training Developer. The developer creates the training based on the designer's plan and vision. The developer takes into consideration such things as the resources that are readily available, the knowledge level of the trainees, the experience level of the trainees, whether the new knowledge and skill can be learned in one class or whether it will take multiple classes, and whether practice is required in order for the trainees to master the new knowledge or skills.

The developer also creates the physical materials that will be used in the training, such as workbooks or handouts for the participants, leader guides for the presenters, and visual presentations such as PowerPoint slides, posters, video, and e-learning courseware. Thanks to technology, this process does not have to be arduous, and many times you can outsource the development of materials. The design and development of training is so crucial to the success of a training program that Chapter Eight is dedicated to expanding these concepts.

Presenter. Often you'll find, as the sole person responsible for training in your organization, you also end up being the presenter of that training; however, you may also use subject matter experts or other credible people within your organization such as managers. If you will do the training yourself, you'll want to be skilled in public speaking, group facilitation, questioning techniques, and time and meeting management. These are also skills that you will want those you may be using as trainers to have as well. For example, if you are using a subject matter expert as a trainer, this person may need coaching in how to respond to questions or how to foster group involvement. An excellent resource for new presenters is *The Instant Trainer* (1998) by C. Leslie Charles and Chris Clarke-Epstein.

Marketer. In the big picture, training is all about change, and most people simply don't like to change. You may find that unless management "forces them," attendees do not readily sign up for training courses. In addition, although management typically understands the value of training, managers frequently believe that they cannot afford to let their employees leave the work area in order to attend training class. Therefore, no matter what other roles you are fulfilling as a trainer, everything you do on a day-to-day basis needs to be infused with a marketing perspective. Marketing the value of your training programs to the entire organization is vital. If you don't sell it, training will disappear because the function will not be valued.

There are three keys to effectively marketing the training department:

1. Create a compelling message.
2. Clearly define what's in it for them.
3. Be proactive and consistent.

Create a Compelling Message. Think of the marketing of your training offerings like a radio or television commercial. If it does not grab people's attention in the first few seconds, they'll never hear the rest of the message. Some ways to grab attention quickly are the use of bright colors (such as printing your registration flyers on neon-colored paper), compelling pictures (such as photos of coworkers attending training), powerful metaphors (remember the public service announcement that showed a frying egg and declared, "This is your brain on drugs"?), and questions, such as the one below. Which of these e-mail announcements for an upcoming training program makes you want to learn more: "Telephone Skills Training" or "Tired of Talking to Angry Customers?"?

Clearly Define What's in It for Them. The question on all potential trainees' minds will be, *What's in it for me?* The question on manager's minds will be similar: *What's in it for my department or the organization?* Your compelling message and all other communications about training offerings should clearly identify the value to be received from the training. For instance, to continue the telephone skills training example, a customer service representative who works in an organization that rates performance on call volume would benefit from the ability to calm angry customers, get to the heart of the problem quickly, and more rapidly conclude the call. The benefit to the manager of the call center would be representatives who handled more calls per hour.

Be Proactive and Consistent. In order for your message to be heard and to compel people to take action (such as signing up for a training class), it must appear frequently and consistently. Consistency in this case relates back to the first key, which is to create a compelling message. It is important, once you decide on the message you want to send to the organization, that you transmit that message consistently, using the same wording and the same "What's in it for me?" messages.

Being proactive goes with being consistent: you cannot be successful by marketing in spurts. Even if you do not have an upcoming training program, the organization as a whole should be hearing from the training department on a consistent basis. You want to eliminate the dilemma that each time you have an offering to announce, it's as if you are reintroducing yourself to the organization. Consider setting up a communication calendar for yourself that ensures that you are marketing the training department on a monthly or weekly basis. Your efforts may be as simple as sending a training tip using broadcast e-mail to the organization, writing an article for the company newsletter, or, if your company allows, sending a broadcast voice mail message to the entire organization on a regular basis. They key is to communicate regularly and with a consistent message.

Another way to market the training function is to create a logo for your department. When the casual clothing retailer Bob's Stores, a division of TJX, wanted to promote the role of human resources and training within the organization, it not only came up with a logo; it renamed itself "The People Place" (Figure 1.1). When the director of training for McDermott, Will and Emery wanted to emphasize the alignment of the training department with the law firm itself, she designed a training department logo that incorporates the law firm's logo as well (Figure 1.2).

FIGURE 1.1. HR AND TRAINING LOGO FOR BOB'S STORES.
Reprinted with permission of Bob's Stores, Meriden, Connecticut.

FIGURE 1.2. TRAINING DEPARTMENT LOGO FOR A LAW FIRM.
Reprinted with permission of McDermott, Will, & Emery, Chicago, Illinois.

> **TIP** ▷ An ambitious trainer who was the only trainer in his organization wanted to make sure that no one forgot him. So he periodically painted his office door a vibrant new color. This tactic kept attention coming his way.

Facilities Manager and Meeting Planner. The administrative tasks of facilities manager may fall to you as well. You may be responsible for making sure that training-related items are ordered and in stock, such as flip charts, markers, projectors, overhead projector bulbs, and pens and pencils for participants who show up with no writing tools. One trainer I know keeps two large plastic tote boxes filled with anything that might be needed in the classroom. Not only will you be responsible for keeping items in stock, but you should take the responsibility for the maintenance of mechanical items such as projectors, TV and VCRs, screens, and stereo systems because it is your effectiveness that will be damaged if the equipment fails.

Trainer's Tool Kit Supplies

Pack a small box or case with the following items so that you are prepared for any emergency that might occur when you are producing a training program:

- Sticky notes of various sizes
- Index cards
- Flip chart markers
- Transparency markers
- Name tents
- Extension cord and power strip
- Three-prong adapter
- Pens, pencils, erasers, and highlighters
- Pencil sharpener
- Masking tape and two-sided tape
- Scissors
- Push pins
- Small stapler
- Tissues
- First aid kit
- Small clock
- Laser pointer

In addition, room reservations, room arrangement, and room comfort may all fall under your purview. Small training departments rarely have a training room to call their own; instead, they must be able to plan far enough ahead so that they can reserve conference rooms, lunchrooms, or unused offices when necessary.

If you've ever sat through a training program or meeting in a room that was icebox cold or hot and stuffy, you understand the importance of room comfort. It is nearly impossible to think when you are too hot or too cold. Be sure you are able to adjust room temperature and lighting yourself when you are choosing the rooms in which to hold your training. If it is impossible to have access to the controls yourself, it's imperative that you become friendly with the person in charge of room comfort; you will find yourself calling on this person often.

If you lack appropriate meeting space at your own facility, you will also be responsible for negotiating contracts with off-site facilities such as hotels and conference facilities. Contract negotiations can involve the cost of the meeting space, what audiovisual equipment is needed, and room arrangement. See Chapter Five for detailed information about meeting planning.

A Classic Challenge

One client with whom I consulted had a group of twelve individuals who needed training on a Web-based software application that had been designed specifically for their company. The company had a computer training room that could accommodate all twelve trainees at once. The original expectation was that the training would be delivered to the group as a whole during two sessions that would be held in the computer training room—until it was discovered that the computers in the training room did not have Internet access (and the IT department was disinclined to give it to us). Luckily, the question of Internet access was asked early enough in the design process to account for this constraint, and the training was instead designed to be done one-on-one, at each individual's desk. Remember your many roles—consultant (ask the right questions) and designer/developer (design the training within the constraints you are given)—and be flexible.

Evaluator. Training is often seen as an expense to the organization because of the time and money that goes into designing, developing, and presenting training. What is not as frequently tracked is the value that is returned as a result of people's new knowledge and skills gained through the training. In order to answer upper management's questions about the value of your training programs, you will need evaluation skills.

There are two important questions when it comes to training evaluation: What is the purpose of the evaluation? and Who cares?

What Is the Purpose of the Evaluation? Evaluation can take many forms. There is a standard for training evaluation known as Kirkpatrick's model; in this model, there are four levels of evaluation that range from, "Did the participants like it?" to "Was it a worthwhile initiative for the company to undertake?" The most basic level, level 1, "Did the participants like it?" is the most typical and the easiest evaluation to conduct. Level 1 evaluations are typically distributed at the end of class and ask participants to express their opinion about the class in terms of content, delivery, materials used, and sometimes even whether the room temperature was comfortable and the food was enjoyable. An example of a level 1 evaluation would be: "On a scale of 1 to 5, how would you rate the instructor's knowledge on the topic?"

Kirkpatrick's Levels of Evaluation
Donald Kirkpatrick developed these four levels of training evaluation in 1954. They are still universally used today:

Level 1: Trainees' reaction
Level 2: Test of knowledge or skill
Level 3: Use of the new knowledge or skill on the job
Level 4: Business results attributable to the training

Level 2 evaluations seek to determine if the participants have learned new knowledge or skills by attending the training program. These evaluations typically take the form of a test for knowledge or performance. For example, a midterm exam in college is a level 2 evaluation that tests what the students have learned during a semester. A driver's license exam is a performance-based level 2 evaluation that seeks to determine if the trainee can successfully operate a vehicle. Level 2 evaluations are typically conducted at the end of the training or soon after and are primarily a snapshot in time; that is, they evaluate what the participant knows or can do at that moment.

Level 3 evaluations are used to determine if the trainees are using their new knowledge and skill back on the job. These types of evaluations may take the form of observations or may be a survey of managers or the trainees themselves to assess how the new skills are being applied on the job. To continue with the driver's license example, while someone might pass the twenty-minute driving test (level 2) by being tested by an instructor, that in no way ensures that they will drive at the speed limit or use their directional signals on a day-to-day basis. But observing them under day-to-day driving conditions, a level 3 evaluation, would let us know if they are truly using the driving skills they were taught.

Level 4 evaluations seek to determine if the training was worthwhile for the company. If a trucking company requires all of its drivers to go through a safety course and in the next six months the number of accidents is reduced or the number of insurance claims falls, it is safe to assume that the safety training did carry over into the workplace and achieved a favorable return for the organization. Level 4 evaluations can be conducted using before and after data that pertain to the behavior you've attempted to change through training. You can find more information about the evaluation of workplace training in the *Handbook of Practical Program Evaluation* by Wholey, Hatry, and Newcomer (2004). Once you've determined what level of evaluation is appropriate for your training program, you'll want to consider who would want to know about the results.

Who Cares? Understanding the types of evaluations you might conduct and when and how to conduct them is not as important as answering the question, Who cares? The various levels of evaluation become increasingly complex, expensive, and time-consuming to implement as you move from level 1 to level 4. Therefore, it's important to know what you will do with the information you gather from the evaluations and who is interested in the results.

If you are seeking to improve your training offerings, then a level 1 or 2 evaluation will give you enough information to adjust things such as the pace of the course, the amount of practice that is allowed during class, or the reference materials used in class. You should be able to conduct level 1 and 2 evaluations with a minimal amount of effort. Level 3 and 4 evaluations, however, will require the cooperation of more individuals within the organization. You may ask a manager to observe his or her workers and report back to you, or you may hold a posttraining focus group of trainees (level 3) to get their impressions once they have had time to practice their newly learned skills on the job. You may also request to see department data or confidential information in order to gauge pre- and posttraining results (level 4). Gathering more data is not necessarily better; as a trainer with limited time and resources, it is a better use of your time to conduct evaluations that you can control yourself.

Unique Needs of an Accidental Trainer

All of the roles and responsibilities just discussed contribute to a varied and exciting career as a trainer. Not every role may apply to your situation; you may find that you have unique challenges depending on how you came to be a trainer. I'll conclude this chapter with some thoughts about specific skills necessary for trainers who play dual roles as human resource specialists, managers, and business owners, or subject matter experts as well as those who have the luxury of being solely focused on training. Each subgroup within the larger accidental trainer group operates within its own unique constraints and access to resources.

Depending on your primary role within the organization—business owner, departmental manager, subject matter expert, or official training department—you may fulfill any of the roles and responsibilities discussed in this chapter to a greater or lesser degree. For instance, a business owner may serve in the capacity of consultant and coach more often than any other role. A full-time trainer may serve in the roles of designer, developer, and marketer more often than any others. And a subject matter expert may concentrate solely on being a presenter. The particular needs of your organization will largely dictate the roles that you fill. I also encourage you to give some thought to what roles you want to perform. One of the ways to be successful as an accidental trainer is to know your strengths and weaknesses and to understand what it is you like and dislike doing, so that you can be most effective with the limited time and resources available to you.

Human Resource Representative, Business Owner, and Manager

The responsibilities and constraints of the HR representative and the business owner or manager are similar in that all three of these groups must fit training into their larger roles and responsibilities. Whether one is responsible for the training of an entire workforce or the professional development of one individual, the responsibility for determining the type and extent of training necessary, and whether the training has an effective impact on the business, can be very time-consuming. The individual manager, business owner, or HR representative is especially eager to find ways to deliver training that are efficient and effective. Chapter Seven will be of particular interest to this group.

Subject Matter Expert

Subject matter experts have a curious mix of possessing the correct information and too much information at the same time. The subject matter expert who is tapped to train others must squeeze training into a small window of opportunity in his day-to-day work. Understanding how others learn and how to present information that aligns with learning styles is important for the subject matter expert to effectively transfer knowledge to others. Chapter Eight will be of particular interest to this group.

The One-Person Department

While the one-person training department has the luxury of concentrating all of his or her energies on the professional development of the workforce, it is a job that can be overwhelming. When you are the only person responsible for a function within the organization, you may find that the requests for training can be more than one person can accommodate. Chapters Six and Seven will be of particular interest to the one-person department.

Summary

While the roles and responsibilities of an accidental trainer are many, you needn't feel overwhelmed. By implementing a daily routine that includes the effective use of resources and time and by implementing the techniques I suggest in the chapters that follow, you'll find yourself on the way to reaping the rewards of the position in no time. The first step is to establish yourself as a credible resource within the organization and to build alliances to help you become successful. These are the topics for Chapter Two.

2

Building Alliances, Marketing the Training Function, and Communicating the Value of Training

IT WILL BE IMPOSSIBLE for you alone to do all the training work that needs to be accomplished in your organization. Also, because you are new to your role, you'll have a lot of questions and the guidance of more experienced trainers and businesspeople. But where do you go for this information? To be successful, it is imperative that you enlist the help of others both within your organization and in your more general professional community. This chapter offers some valuable suggestions that will enable you to build relationships both internally and externally.

Building Alliances

One of the best ways to quickly be effective in your new training role is to build a support system for yourself. The support system can and should include both internal resources, such as co-workers and management, and external resources, such as fellow trainers and managers from other industries or businesses in your geographical area.

Building Alliances Within Your Organization

Just because you don't have a formal training function inside your organization doesn't mean that you have nowhere to turn for internal support. There are a number of ways to build valuable relationships within your company immediately and also more time-consuming and methodical approaches to building alliances.

Networking. Most people don't think about the opportunity of networking within their own company. However, if you are the newly designated trainer, even if you have worked for the company in another capacity, it's essential to start building relationships in your new role. One of the easiest and smartest places to start is by meeting individually with each department manager. In general, people won't think to reach out to you because you are new in your position and they may not have any idea what your purpose is, so it's up to you to make the first contact.

A simple twenty- or thirty-minute meeting in which you ask, "What are the challenges facing your department?" communicates that you are ready to assist. In addition to asking about problems, ask them to talk to you about the core processes of their departments (what they do, how they get it done, how long it typically takes) and the typical job tasks that an individual in the department might perform. If you are meeting with upper-level managers, ask them about their general organizational philosophies. Where do they see the company going in the next three to five years? What is the one thing about the business that keeps them up at night? If they could choose to add head count or increase the skills of the current workforce, which would they choose? This last question is particularly helpful because if they choose skills, your follow-on question will then be, "What skills should the current workforce develop, in your opinion?"

In addition to meeting individually with department managers, ask permission to sit in on one of their regularly scheduled departmental meetings.

Do not ask to be placed on the agenda, and do not attend the meeting with any preconceived notions about how you can help the department. Simply sit quietly through the meeting and observe. This type of background knowledge will serve you well in the future if you are asked to provide training for the department. Finally, talk with the people who do the work in each department. Many times you'll find that the manager's perspective of people's abilities or the work they do is not in alignment with the workers' perspectives. In Chapter Eight we will discuss the significance of analyzing whether training is truly needed. For now, remember this important point: it is always important to balance the realities of the workers' lives with the expectations of management.

When I am called in to an organization because management believes there's a training need, I typically alert my clients, "For the first few days [or weeks], it may look as if I'm doing nothing." This is because I am gathering the type of information discussed earlier. It's important to have a sense of how the business truly operates, which can be at odds with how management or the organization as a whole would like to see it operate. One of our jobs as trainers is to align these two realities as closely as possible.

Another important way to establish relationships with others, is akin to the theory "management by walking around." This theory proposes that you'll learn more about your organization by being out in it than you will by sitting behind a desk in your office. It is important that you are visible. Just as workers can be suspicious or worried when a new manager arrives, the same can be true when there is a new trainer or a training department is created. You want everyone within the organization to understand that your sole mission is to improve the organization and that you are approachable by anyone. In addition to walking through the various production areas on a daily basis, try "working the lunchroom." The lunchroom or an unofficial break area (for instance, where the smokers gather) are good places to network informally because most people are relaxed and happy to speak with you. Be careful that you do not turn networking into a fact-finding mission; you don't want people to feel that every time you approach them, you expect information or are prodding for details. Rather, simply connect with people on a personal level, and you'll discover many things about the operating structure of your organization.

Finally, as you are networking, be sure to subtly transmit the philosophy that training is everyone's responsibility. Training will not be effective unless everyone, from the CEO to the individual on the assembly line, understands his or her role in making it effective. Rather than saying, "I'll see what *I* can do about that" or "I'll put that on *my* list," use inclusive language: "I'd like to *help you* with that" or "Let's talk further so *we* can see how we might best address that."

Picking Low-Hanging Fruit. When you are trying to change the way a business operates by implementing a training intervention, it's best to start with the easy wins, or, as salespeople like to refer to an easy sale, "low-hanging fruit." Once you have done a sufficient amount of networking, you'll have a good understanding of who within the organization would most benefit from your assistance and who would be most welcome to receiving it: these are the low-hanging departmental fruit that are ready for your first interventions. Start with them. When they do well as a result, their success will reflect well on you, and you will have created a happy ally. As you begin to have success with the easy wins, other departments and individuals who may have been resistant to a training solution will begin to come around.

One of the primary ways to make a manager or a department look good is by linking the training that you provide to the business objectives of that department. When you are conducting your initial networking meetings or when you are called in because a manager perceives a training need, one of the most crucial questions you should ask is, "What will be the impact of this training on the business?" Linking your training to the goals and objectives of the department helps to ensure that the results of your training will be positive and visible, outcomes that can result in allies who weren't even part of the training. Consider a chief financial officer who is the pleased recipient of properly prepared reports because you have trained the audit department.

Finally, a way in which you can link your networking and your allies together is to begin to identify individuals who would like a more active role in developing and delivering training. You'll find many individuals who would love the opportunity to share their knowledge with others as instructors. Others will welcome the chance to develop new skills, such as public speaking or group facilitation, or simply to do something new and challenging within their current position. As you begin to establish the roles and responsibilities of your training function, keep in mind those individuals you encounter who express an interest in training; you might be able to use them as an auxiliary training staff in the future.

Creating Task Forces and Advisory Committees

Forming task forces and advisory committees will require a more coordinated effort between training and the organization as a whole. They are also ongoing commitments for those involved. These are the more time-consuming approaches to building alliances. As the coordinator for each group, you'll need to plan agendas, issue meeting minutes, follow up on action items, and fulfill other requirements of running an ongoing committee. For these reasons, you may not wish to start a task force or advisory committee until you have been in your position for a few months and fully understand how you might use each to best advantage in assisting you.

It's more than likely that unless you are the owner of the business, you do not possess a complete understanding of how your company operates. One way to build alliances throughout the organization is to make it your mission to understand the business, its leadership, its culture, and how it approaches learning. You can begin learning more about the business by reading the reports and regular communications that the company issues. If your company is publicly traded, be sure to get a copy of its annual report; if your company conducts customer satisfaction surveys, these would be helpful background information for you as well. And in your one-on-one meetings with managers and department heads, ask whether they have conducted any surveys about employee satisfaction or desired training needs. If so, get copies of these as well.

> **TIP** ▷ You can obtain annual reports from your investor relations department or from http://www.sec.gov/edgar.

One common complaint voiced about training practitioners is that we typically are not "business people." We are more "people people." You can forestall this reputation for yourself by making sure that you understand and can support your company's business goals and can speak about them intelligently. You can also invite management to be the guiding force behind training decisions (people rarely argue with something they had a hand in creating) and you will demonstrate that you are making business needs the priority of the training department.

Creating a Management Task Force. In order to get a better sense of the leadership culture of your organization and how that leadership might feel about learning, start a management task force. To begin, schedule a meeting with no more than five managers who understand the importance of training and for whom training will have the most impact. These managers may not be direct recipients of the training, but they might be beneficiaries of or affected by it. For example, the shipping department may not receive the training, but because of training that is given to the order processing department, the workload of the shipping department may change. The manager of the shipping department will most likely want to be involved in the decision making regarding the training for the order processing group.

Once you have conducted your individual meetings with managers, you can bring a list of suggested training areas (such as the incoming sales group) or topics (such as "closing the sale") to your first management task force meeting. By allowing the task force to weigh and discuss the importance of the various potential training initiatives, you'll begin to understand more clearly the priorities of your company. You will also have a greater chance of ensuring that the training you create and deliver will be aligned with the goals of the business. It's safe to assume your task force will choose topics that are important to the success of the business because you will have given a number of individuals, who may have competing goals, an equal voice in the training agenda.

There are two crucial benefits to forming and conducting management task force meetings. The first is that you never have to agonize over what training should be tackled first. Your task force has become your pseudo-boss and will make those decisions for you. The second benefit is that you will not have to struggle with management buy-in or support, since it is management that decided the focus of the training and empowered you to make it happen.

Here are some tips to effectively using a management task force:

- Hold meetings no more than once a month but no less than once every six weeks.

- Hold breakfast meetings because they seem to be the best-attended time of the day. It is less likely that your committee members will find their schedules have filled up if you get to them first thing in the morning.

- Schedule the meeting for forty-five minutes or less. Getting an hour on someone's calendar is difficult, but requests for less than an hour are usually granted.

- Have no more than five task force members; however, you can rotate membership on the task force every six or twelve months. In fact, it is recommended that you do replace members on a yearly basis, so that different areas of the business can be heard.

If you have a company cafeteria, request that the group meet there; if you have no such relaxed meeting area available, invite them to a conference room and provide light refreshments. Although providing refreshments will take a bit of money out of your budget, you'll find that people are more relaxed and less in a hurry to move on to their next task. The returns are exponential when you consider the support that you'll have from upper management as well as the clear guidance you will receive on what your priorities should be for the coming month or quarter.

Finally, be sure to share both good news and the bad whenever you meet with your task force. You will have struggles, and you will undoubtedly face failures as you begin to establish the role of training in your organization. Consistently behaving as if all is well will undermine your credibility with the task force when you inevitably face a hurdle that may require their intervention or support. Because you are a new department or new to the field of training, you'll slowly begin to find what works and what doesn't work for your organization. Sharing your thoughts and concerns with your task force will reinforce to them that you are focused on doing what is best for the business.

Creating an Advisory Committee. An advisory committee is similar to a management task force, but it is made up of frontline workers in the organization. Like the management task force, it is important to have representation from across the organization and from all levels, from hourly workers to supervisors. For example, if you want store managers to conduct new hire training, it's a good idea to have input from store management, supervisors, frontline workers, and back-office workers. They will provide their thoughts on how the training should be delivered and what should be accomplished by the conclusion of it. An advisory committee should have no more than thirteen members, and the membership seats should be rotated regularly. Larger groups can be harder to facilitate, and you want to be sure everyone has an equal chance to participate in the discussion. You'll find that you have to do much less marketing of the training function when you have thirteen ambassadors who return to their work areas every month understanding that they are responsible in part for the success of their organization.

Building Alliances Outside the Organization

Relationships with people who are external to your company are valuable because they will look at your situation in a different light and undoubtedly offer a different perspective. I also feel it's important to have external relationships with professional peers for those times when you are second-guessing yourself or you just want to sound off. An external supporter will listen objectively (and chuckle) when you say something like, "They want this training rolled out in three weeks! They're nuts!" An internal supporter, hearing the same exclamation, might wonder, "Is she going to undermine this training?

What if it doesn't get done in time?" To build alliances, look to industry organizations, professional organizations, and your local chamber of commerce.

Industry Organizations. Industry organizations are where you will get the most accurate information and feedback about how your industry is implementing training. You'll be able to ask other training professionals in your industry segment about the results they achieved when they implemented training on a particular topic, and in addition, you'll get a sense of what the industry overall feels is important in terms of developing the workforce for the industry. For example, *Maintenance Solutions,* the trade publication of the facilities management industry, includes a semimonthly column regarding training needs and priorities. The October 2004 edition included an article titled "Training Spotlight: Electrical Systems," which states, "Safety training is a continuous effort that is best done with frequent, short, job-related meetings," and continues, "Safe work performance begins with each technician knowing the personal protective equipment (PPE) he or she should wear and how to adjust and wear it correctly." If you work in the facilities management industry, you don't have to identify what training is essential or even what content should be covered in the training; your industry is doing it for you! In addition to having knowledge about the training needs of the industry, joining industry groups and having contacts within the industry may save you from having to reinvent the wheel; of course, you'll want to validate that an industry need is indeed a need for your organization as well.

A project with a state department of transportation required the design of training in such topics as basic road construction, drainage, and surveying. I found it hard to imagine that my client was the only state that had ever needed to provide that type of training to its workforce. Before putting pen to paper (or fingers to keyboard), I requested that my client call every state commissioner of transportation across the United States to see if they had faced a similar challenge and what they had done to address it. Two states sent us their training programs with permission to use what we needed. What a time saver!

Belonging to an industry organization will provide you with a kind of support that you will not receive anywhere else. You can find industry organizations by using a search engine. Type the name of your industry and the word *association* into the search field. For example, a search on *telecommunications association* returned, among many others, the National Cable & Telecommunications Association, Canadian Wireless Telecommunications Association, and Industrial Telecommunications Association.

Professional Training Organizations. Professional training organizations are important because this is where you will be able to hone your skills as a trainer. There are a number of professional associations, such as the American Society for Training and Development, the International Society for Performance Improvement, and the Organization Development Network, that deal specifically with workplace training. These types of organizations will not provide information or best practices about how to implement training in your particular industry, but they will be beneficial in that you will be able to rub elbows with other training professionals so that you can enhance your knowledge and skills about the field of training in general.

> **TIP**
>
> American Society for Training and Development,
>   http://www.astd.org
> International Society for Performance Improvement,
>   http://www.ispi.org
> Organization Development Network,
>   http://www.ODnetwork.org

Chamber of Commerce. Join your local chamber of commerce or begin attending their events if your business already is a member. The benefit derived from chamber membership is that it will put you in touch with other businesses in your area who may be facing the same kind of challenges that you are—and may have already figured out the solution. Because chambers foster a sense of "businesspeople helping other businesspeople," you will find an easy flow of information and generous assistance whenever you might need it. For instance, you may find that your local bank is providing first-line supervisory training through a consultant who will come to the bank five times over the course of the next two months to provide the training. Your company would benefit from the same type of training, but you don't have the budget to hire the consultant. Suggest to your bank contact that you be allowed to send a certain number of your employees at a per head cost, or for some portion of the consultant's fee. You both win: the bank saves money and you are able to offer training that you otherwise would not have been able to provide.

All three of the external resources just mentioned have the additional benefit of introducing you to area professionals. Each of these types of organizations will have local chapters near you and more than likely will hold monthly networking and professional development opportunities for a nominal cost. Not only will you be immersing yourself in industry standards and developing your own professional skills, but you will be able to develop a network of local resources that you can call on when you're feeling isolated or stumped by your job.

Being a part-time or one-person department doesn't mean you have to work alone. Build alliances internally by networking and creating management and worker advisory committees that will guide you in your work. Building external alliances in your professional and local community will assist you when you need more global expertise about the field of training or how training is carried out in your industry. These alliances will help you to do your job more easily and efficiently and will allow you to accomplish more than you ever could by working alone. The next two sections will assist you with formulating and dispersing communications about the training department that will help get your work noticed and to communicate its value to the organization.

Marketing the Training Function

If you don't sell it, training can simply disappear. Marketing your training initiatives is essential to gain management buy-in and support and encourage employee participation in training. Almost all marketing approaches boil down to one thing: positive, informative communication. In Chapter One I discussed how to create and start to disseminate your marketing message by applying these three steps:

1. Create a compelling message.

2. Clearly define what's in it for them.

3. Be proactive and consistent.

Now I'll provide some specific vehicles to engage your audience and create your marketing campaign.

Columns or Tips

If your company already has an internal newsletter, speak with the editor about writing a regular training column. If no such newsletter already exists, you can easily begin your own e-newsletter using your internal e-mail system. Ensure that anything sent from the training department is engaging and helpful in performing one's job; don't just send a calendar of events. Training tips might be about software applications, management practices, or on-the-job-skills that are unique to your organization. Keep the tips short and how-to oriented so that recipients clearly see the value of reading your e-newsletter. (See the newsletter sample in the box.) You can start with a helpful tip and then provide a calendar of upcoming events. This format helps to ensure that your messages get opened (because one never knows what this week's helpful tip will be), and once recipients begin reading, your hope is that they will read the entire message, including the calendar of events.

> **TIP** Two good resources for tips are the Microsoft Office Web page (http://office.microsoft.com) (for software tips), and the Dummies site (http://www.Dummies.com), which allows you to subscribe to weekly e-mail tips on a myriad of topics.

Newsletter Sample

Tips from Training

This Week's Tip: Transferring Large Files via E-Mail

Need to send a file to yourself at home so you can work over the weekend—but it's too big to get through to the in-box of your personal e-mail service? Or maybe you need to send a user manual with screen shots to a customer whose e-mail system won't accept the large file size. Try http://www.yousendit.com/.

This amazing site lets you attach a file up to 1 Gig to any e-mail recipient. You Send It stores the file on their server and then sends a link, via e-mail, to the recipient. All you need are two different e-mail addresses: yours and the recipient's. Brilliant!

Upcoming Training Sessions

- Time Management: Tuesday the 16th, 2:00–4:00 P.M. Gray Conference Room, 3rd floor. Only 5 seats left!

- Introduction to Six Sigma: Come find out what it's all about and voice your opinion about implementing Six Sigma practices here at [our company]. Friday the 19th, 1:00–2:00 with guest speaker Professor John Oxley from Northeast College.

- Second Offering Added! The last CSR Telephone Skills session, presented by Tricia Tolles, "sold out" in less than a week, so we've added another session. Reserve the date on your calendar now (and call the Training Department at ext. 662 or reply to this e-mail to reserve your spot).

    When: Tuesday March 22

    Time: 9:00 A.M.–4:00 P.M. (lunch will be 12:00–1:30 and is not provided)

    Agenda: Visit the training department online for the complete agenda; www.ourcompany.com/training.CSR_Agenda.html

Showcase Success Stories

As your training offerings roll out, you can write short success stories for pub-lication in the company newsletter. You'll want to include the type of training offered, why it was offered (a description of the problem it was to address), who attended (for instance, the second-shift supervisors), and how the atten-dees are now implementing their new skills back on the job. Be sure to include quotations or accolades from attendees (collect them on your evaluation sheets, which is addressed in Chapter Eight), and whenever possible, take pictures as the training is being conducted. Think about the design of newspapers or mag-azines you read: pictures draw attention, and first-person accounts make the story more personal. Incorporate these techniques to make your segments in the newsletter attention getting. You can achieve the same effect (but proba-bly reach fewer people) by posting your tips or success stories on a prominent bulletin board. The bulletin boards that are most likely to be read are usually found in the cafeteria, the break room, or by the time clock. Another option is to create a training showcase outside your office. In effect, you are creating your own bulletin board. With time, people will come to look at your show-case as a way to find out what's happening in the training department.

Offer a Pilot or Preview

A pilot is a test offering that will allow your potential audience to gauge the value of the training. It may be the full-blown course or a selected excerpt from the course. A representative sample of your targeted audience attends the training and evaluates it. By offering a pilot, you allow management to withhold endorsement of the training until the test group has been polled for their feelings and business outcomes have been evaluated. The course is refined based on the feedback from the pilot, before it is rolled out to the larger group. This wait-and-see approach will be typical if the training offer-ing will be costly or time-consuming to roll out.

Many times it's valuable to offer a preview of the training to management so that they can better understand what the content will be, as well as offer their thoughts on refining it if necessary. A preview typically involves a review of the training course with an in-depth explanation of how the topics will be delivered. It is not as thorough as a pilot. For instance, you might say, "From

1:00 to 3:00 P.M., participants will role-play closing the sale." You would not actually demonstrate or conduct the role-play activity. The preview may last anywhere from an hour to a day, depending on the overall length of the training offering.

If you're having trouble getting training to be accepted within the organization, try offering a preview or offer to make a "guest appearance" at a regularly scheduled departmental meeting. Many times managers cannot see the value in letting their employees leave the work area for two or four hours or more. If you are able to attend a regular departmental meeting and offer just fifteen minutes of your best hard-hitting, use-it-on-the-job-*today* content, you may have a better chance of attracting both the manager and the workers to the complete course.

> **TIP** A preview, pulled from a full-day project management course, might offer an easy-to-understand explanation of the use of GANTT charts.

I assisted in designing a training preview that was a full-day offering presenting a synopsis of a five-day curriculum. The attendees were regional managers from across the United States who would be sending their sales managers to the training. The materials given to the regional managers included the workbooks and the tools that the participants would be using throughout the training. The preview was delivered by the two instructors who would ultimately be delivering the course. The value of offering this type of preview was that the regional managers endorsed the content, contributed to the ultimate business outcomes they wanted to see the training address, and were confident in sending their sales managers for an entire week of training. The regional managers probably thought we were attempting to gain their input and approval; in reality we were marketing the class to them. Without the preview, which helped them to see the value of the training and be comfortable with it, it is questionable whether they would have let their sales managers leave the field for an entire week.

Getting the word out is critical to getting people to training events. After all, an empty training room does not improve the organization's performance. Sometimes, however, marketing specific initiatives is not enough. In an organization with a fledgling training culture, you need to start early and let people know that training is a valuable investment in time and resources.

Communicating the Value of Training

When training is done well, it is often not recognized. In many respects you can liken it to a customer service experience: poor customer service experiences are much more memorable than good ones. A good customer service experience is deemed normal or expected. In order for training to be understood as a wise business investment within your organization, it behooves you to communicate the value of training because you can't rely on satisfied attendees to do it (a good experience may be unremarkable). Do not sit passively by, hoping that your internal customers will surely recognize the contribution your work is making to the organization. When the economy slows down, as it always does, training is always one of the first items to be cut, primarily because those who work in training do a terrible job of communicating their value. If you're going to take on the role of trainer, do your job well, and communicate its success to the rest of the organization.

With Whom Should You Be Communicating?

Everyone within the organization should be apprised of what the training department is doing and how it is contributing to the goals of the organization. What is communicated and with whom can be segmented into three primary interest groups—senior-level management, managers, and workers—and what you communicate to each is slightly different.

Senior-Level Management. Senior-level managers are those individuals who have the term *senior* or *chief* in their title (such as senior vice president, chief executive officer, chief financial officer). It is this layer of management that is more typically concerned with setting the vision and direction of the organization as a whole. It is rare that you'll see this level of individual in your training classes, so it is important that you keep them apprised of what the training department is accomplishing on behalf of the organization.

Managers. Managers within a typical organization will have the term *manager* or *director* in their title (such as customer service manager, director of quality assurance). These individuals will also rarely be seen in your training classes. It is a fairly typical occurrence, especially within an organization introducing a training department, that management is exempt from training. Interestingly, it is this layer of management that has the most direct working relationship with the majority of individuals who do attend training, yet they are often not fully apprised of what occurs in the training classes or what their role should be in supporting the new knowledge and skills once their workers return to the job. You might think that the customer service manager would inherently see the value of sending customer service representatives to training, but unfortunately, value is invisible. Unless you specifically bring it to someone's attention, it will undoubtedly go unnoticed.

Workers. The workers, or the line and staff individuals who make up the largest population of any organization, are also the individuals who will attend the majority of training classes. Again, it is easy to assume that this group would readily see the value of attending training. They come to a training class, learn new skills, and return to their jobs better able to do their work. Who would not see the value in that? In the previous chapter, I addressed the fact that training more often than not means change to individuals, and most people don't like to move out of their comfort zone even if a new way of conducting themselves would make their lives easier. This is your audience. Therefore, the third significant population to whom you should be communicating the value of training is the workers themselves.

What to Communicate, and How

The prospect of creating a formal communication plan may seem overwhelming, and rightfully so. Your likely argument is that "no one will hear it or see it or read it" anyway. But without a formalized plan, your communications will be haphazard at best and perhaps contradictory at their worst. Your goal should be for the organization as a whole to hear positive and compelling things about training, and the only way to ensure that is to create those communications yourself. This section offers tips on what to communicate and how to communicate it.

Written Communications.   On a regular basis you will want to issue some formal communications from the training department. At a minimum, formal communications should include memos, briefings, and executive summaries. Issuing each type of communication by e-mail will allow recipients to easily save and refer back to your communications.

Memos.   Memos should be issued once a month to all senior management and management positions. The subject line for the communication might be "training memo" or "training update." Keep the communication short (no more than three or four paragraphs) and upbeat. Include what the training department is currently working on that will roll out in the future and what the training department has accomplished during the month. Although you don't want the memo to overwhelm recipients with numbers or statistics (don't tell them how many people were trained or how many hours of training took place), you do want to include positive numbers that are attributable to training, such as increased customer satisfaction scores, reduced cycle time, or the number of accident-free days. The close of the training memo should always invite individuals to contact you if they have any questions or would like further information. This will allow you and your department to regularly present itself in a consistently positive light and will reinforce that the training department is approachable and happy to assist anyone within the organization. A training update might also be included in a company newsletter or posted on a common bulletin board. If you are able to issue the memo in a hard copy, print format, be sure to include photos of recent training events. Photos always capture attention and cause people to read the caption that explains the photo.

Briefings.   A briefing should be used when you would like to communicate new findings or information about the field of training to nonsenior management and the influencers in your organization. Briefings should also be kept to no more than a few paragraphs. Perhaps you will issue a briefing after having attended a conference or after having researched a topic. The training briefing might discuss industry statistics and how your organization compares, it might profile what a competitor is doing in terms of workforce development, or it might discuss governmental issues affecting your company and how training can contribute to compliance. The purpose of a briefing is to remind those individuals with influence that you are staying current with the pulse of the training industry and constantly evaluating how trends in the industry might affect your own organization.

Executive Summaries. Finally, an executive summary can be issued to all levels of management, including line supervisors, who may be affected by a particular training. Because managers are frequently exempt from training, they may be at a loss as to how to reinforce the new knowledge and skills their workers have acquired because they do not know what the training covered. Executive summaries should include:

- A high-level overview about what is contained in the training
- How the training may affect the functioning of the department, such as the fact that queue time might be longer in the customer service department on days when training occurs because a number of the representatives will be off the floor
- What new skills the participants will be introduced to
- How the new skills will apply to their job
- What management and supervisors can do to help ensure that the participants are able to apply their new skills once they return to their jobs (such as allowing extra production time while trainees become proficient at their new skills)
- How the new skills will apply to the future of the company (for example, "Our company has set reduced time-to-market as a goal; therefore this quality assurance training has been developed in order to . . . ")

This last point can be more broadly viewed as speaking with another voice. For example, if you do not have a specific company goal to align the training with, you might say, "Customer feedback has told us that we need XYZ training," or, "Evaluations conducted after new salespeople have been on the job for six months point to these additional skills as critical." Using this "other" voice reinforces that the training department is consistently working to improve the organization by focusing on critical and documented training needs. An executive summary should be issued approximately one week before a new training program is rolled out so that the managers of trainees are prepared for a change in performance and can begin to think about how they will support it in the worker's day-to-day activities.

Spoken Communications

Every day you will need to talk with others about the training function. Sometimes you will have scheduled formal presentations, but most often you will find yourself in impromptu situations where you will need to answer questions, communicate the value of training, or defend a decision you have made. When this happens, it's important to sound confident and prepared, and not to fumble with your words. Here are some tips.

Use Their Language. People are more likely to listen to your communications if they believe you are speaking about them or speaking their language. One way to determine what "language" someone speaks is to simply look at the person's title—for instance, *return on investment* is important to a finance manager but probably means little to the customer service manager. The customer service manager would be more influenced by a communication that focused on increased customer satisfaction or a reduced number of calls being escalated to supervisors. Another way to determine "language" is to listen when individuals describe problems or concerns associated with their business unit. For instance, you would naturally assume a quality control manager would be concerned with quality control issues, but you may not know the production manager is also worried about quality control unless you had a conversation with him about what was going on in his department. A third, and so obvious it is almost always overlooked, way to learn what others care about is to ask them. The next time you run into someone, try: "The last time we spoke, you were concerned [or excited] about . . . How's that going?" By paraphrasing a person's concerns and using her language when you speak with her, you will earn a reputation within your organization as someone who understands what is needed to advance the business.

Use Stories. Stories are powerful communication tools because people tend to remember a story more than they remember facts and figures. If you are going to communicate training success, be sure to also include stories about trainees who have had personal success. For example, in addition to saying, "As a result of the customer service training, the call center queue time has been reduced from an average of three minutes to an average of seventy seconds," be sure to also say, "and Roger P. was personally singled out by the IT manager of our client company, MediaZach, for his personable and professional handling of a service issue." This type of illustration communicates the message: the customers notice (and benefit from) our investment in training.

Personal Communications. When you run into a manager or other person of influence in the cafeteria or in the elevator, try to interject a formal pronouncement about training along with your informal conversation about the weather or your weekend plans. For example, when parting company, you might say, "I'm glad I ran into you. I'm on my way to poke my head into the quality assurance training happening in training room C. The early buzz we're hearing about this class is that the participants are eager to apply it back on the job." This type of value communication subtly reminds the other party of what the training department is doing on behalf of the organization. Keep your message short and consistent and, if at all possible, tailored to the interests of the other party. So a parting communication with the finance manager might sound a little different: "I'm glad I ran into you. I'm on my way to poke my head into the quality assurance training happening in training room C. Based on the feedback I'm hearing from this class, I really think we're going to see a significant reduction in time to market—maybe as much as a day."

Personal communications are always more valued and welcomed than written memos. When possible, ask to make a short presentation at staff or project meetings, and always take the time to have one-on-one conversations when you informally bump into interested individuals from all ranks within your organization.

Summary

Even if you are working independently, that does not mean you are alone. A large part of your new job is to create alliances inside and outside your organization. Once the alliances are created, maintain those relationships by marketing your initiatives and constantly reinforcing the value of the service you are providing. Consistency is key to your success. Communicating the value of training is a continuous process. By following the suggestions in this chapter and scheduling regular communications, you'll make certain that you are in control of the image of training. Communicating the activities and results of training in brief and consistent ways will ensure that the organization understands your contributions rather than leaving them to draw their own conclusions about the value of training.

3

Identifying Training Needs, Determining a Budget for Them, and Proving Their Worth

TRAINING IS OFTEN seen as a cost center or expenditure by organizations because it's difficult to assign a one-to-one correlation between training dollars that are invested and the return that the company sees. It is not impossible to make this correlation—there's an entire industry focused on the return on investment associated with training—but the prevailing opinion is that the training department is a cost center. View your organization's investment in training as you would view an investment in a college education. Sometimes there's no immediate return and sometimes it's impossible to put your finger on the value, but there is no arguing with the fact that a college education makes a positive contribution to an individual's future.

TIP ▷ According to the U.S. Census, a college graduate with a bachelor's degree earns nearly $1 million more over his or her lifetime than a high school graduate does.

The focus of this chapter is not on accounting. Rather, its goal is to assist you in determining how much money you may need to allot to an overall training budget or a given training program. More important, this chapter will assist you in supporting your requests for training dollars. I believe how you budget is not as important as understanding what you should consider when creating or requesting a budget. This chapter addresses gathering information that will help you to pinpoint your budget needs so that you can have a ball-park number to work with and discusses how to prove the value of training.

Common Financial Terms

Although you don't have to be an accounting whiz to budget for training, it is helpful to have an understanding of the financial terms you might come across as you work with budgeting:

Charge back: The process of charging departments that use your training. For example, a course on finance for nonfinancial managers would cost a certain amount per attendee for each department that sends someone.

Cost-benefit analysis: Similar to ROI. Sometimes used in advance of an expenditure to determine if the expenditure would be worthwhile.

Cost center: A unit or department for which operating costs are accumulated or calculated.

Cost per head: A typical way for training expenditures to be calculated. For example, if a training course costs $18,000 in total and thirty-two people attend the training, the cost per head is $562.50.

Fixed costs: An expense that will be constant despite the number of programs offered, the number of participants that attend, and other variables. Examples are the cost of a video or the cost of membership in a professional organization.

Income statement, P&L: Presents the sales, expenses, and profit or loss of a business. Used interchangeably.

Indirect costs: Associated more with facilities or administrative items such as the cost of electricity or the cost of a training room standing empty three out of five days.

Licensed materials: When purchasing materials or courses from a vendor, licenses are sometimes purchased. These may be one time, subscription, or on a per head basis.

Per diem: Literally translated as "for the day." A typical way for consultants to charge for expenses to be reimbursed. The Internal Revenue Service's standard per diem rates for various cities is available at http://www.irs.gov/pub/irs-pdf/p1542.pdf/.

ROI: Return on investment. How much an expenditure on training has returned to the company in tangible and intangible benefits.

T&E: Stands for Travel and Expenses associated with a certain program (after the fact) or budgeted for a specific program or department.

Before you can budget for training, you'll need to have an idea of what training is needed within your organization. Armed with the right information, you can create, justify, and manage your budget more precisely.

Gathering Data

If your organization feels that it is important to offer training without necessarily creating a full-time training function, a key activity for you will be to gather company data to validate the amount of money that should be allotted for individual training initiatives rather than assemble a training budget. In order to accomplish this, you'll want to get a sense of how much training the organization will need in the coming year. This section provides some ideas on where to gather this information. Note that you are not seeking monetary figures; rather, you are seeking to identify training needs that will require a budget.

Company Goals Can Herald Training Needs

One of the first places to look for potential training needs is at your company's planned initiatives for the coming year. Perhaps a new product is being introduced and therefore product knowledge training will be required for the customer service and help desk representatives, as well as the internal and external sales force. Or perhaps your company is planning to increase production—say, by starting a second shift—which would require not only new hire orientation (training) but also on-the-job skills training. This could be a rather large endeavor, but it also would be completed in a defined period of time.

You'll also benefit from inquiring about managers' or organizational goals. Perhaps one of the goals for your company in the coming year is to reduce the cost of its insurance premiums. This may not sound like a training need, but what if the high insurance premiums are in part a result of a large number of accidents by your fleet drivers? The premiums may be reduced by providing safety training to the drivers who work for your company.

When speaking with managers and senior leaders, ask if they think training can assist them in reaching their planned goals. In addition to the narrow focus of your company, you'll also want to be aware of any industry or governmental regulations that may affect your company and require training, such as Occupational Safety and Health Administration regulations, ISO9000 (and beyond), the U.S. Patriot Act, or the PhRMA Code.

Departmental Data

Each department within the organization probably has its own business plan and goals for the year. These individual plans direct the departments in support of the organization's overall plan. You'll want to gather data from these departments. The easiest approach is to send a survey to all of the department managers asking them what training classes they would like to offer their workers in the coming year; however, this method may not yield any useful responses unless you control the types of responses you'll get. Rather than asking, "What do you need?" ask, "Do you need this?" If you offer a number of suggestions from which the departmental managers can choose, you'll have a list of training programs that managers deem to have the most importance overall. The suggestions may be based on the company goals, or they may be in generic categories such as sales training, customer service training, or financial skills. People tend to have an easier time responding to suggestions than they do creating ideas from scratch.

Individual Requests

Be prepared for requests that may come from individuals who want to develop their knowledge or skills in a particular area. For instance, the customer service department may determine that its customer data would be more easily managed by using a particular software, but only one or two individuals from the company would need to have training in this program.

TIP When planning your budget, don't forget your own professional development. It's important that you keep abreast of what is happening in the field of training and performance improvement so that you can bring the best ideas and services to your own organization. Some items you may want to budget for include:

- Professional association memberships. These can range from $50 to $500.
- Subscriptions to journals and newsletters. These can range from $30 to $150.
- Attendance at at least one conference per year that is either training related or specific to your industry. These can range from $295 to $2,995, which is just for the cost of the conference; you will also need to budget for travel, lodging, and meals.

You may be able to gain awareness of individual needs like this by surveying the departmental managers; however, you may also want to conduct a survey of the employees within the organization to see what types of professional development they are interested in. Remember that at this point, you are not assigning any dollar amounts to requests; rather, you are trying to get a sense of the training needs that may develop in the future. In this regard, the more information you have, the better.

Aligning Training with Goals to Help Ensure Funding

In this era of limited resources, a company always wants to be sure that it is getting value for the dollars it spends. Rarely do organizations have sufficient funds to cover all of their desired plans. Therefore, whenever you are requesting a budget for training offerings, be sure that you can substantiate how the training aligns with the company's goals. Rather than defending your dollar requests, you will be focusing on the potential return for the organization. For example, a food processing plant was quoted fifty-six thousand dollars for the development of new hire training that covered the safe and proper way to handle the raw material food product through the various stages of inspection, processing, and packaging. When the operations manager requesting the training was asked to validate the expenditure, he was able to cite savings in terms of reduced employee turnover, fewer on-the-job accidents, fewer Occupational Safety and Health Administration violations, and less wasted food product resulting from human errors in the processing.

By aligning training initiatives with business goals, you'll be able to say, "This is the impact [or return] the training will have on XYZ department," rather than having to defend a request for money.

Proving the Value of Training

The motivational speaker Zig Ziglar, has a classic anecdote about employee training:

What's worse than training your employees and losing them?
Not training them and keeping them.

One of the ways I like to prove the value of training is by asking, "What is the cost of *not* doing the training?" Managers and business owners sometimes gasp at what they perceive to be the high cost of a training initiative. This is especially true when they cannot see a tangible deliverable in return for the money invested. For instance, a sales training class delivered to twenty participants at a cost of eighteen thousand dollars can seem like a lot of money. But if that sales training results in five new sales in the next two months and each of those sales is worth five thousand dollars, the training has then returned seven thousand dollars to the organization.

When requesting a budget for training initiatives, a useful exercise is to determine what it would cost the company not to provide the training at all. In addition to increasing sales, training can help to reduce turnover, assist in lowering accidents and injuries on the job, and increase quality and efficiency. In short, training can produce returns that far exceed the cost of training.

A manufacturer of printed circuit boards was forced to stop production and send its production workers home because one crucial piece of machinery malfunctioned and a replacement part would take forty-eight hours to arrive. The machinery failed because the machine's operator failed to do preventive maintenance and inspection. The company had been considering creating a preventive maintenance training program and schedule for the manufacturing floor, but had not yet done so. The failure conservatively cost the manufacturer twenty thousand dollars in parts, delayed production, and salaries that had to be paid even though no work was being done.

One obstacle that training departments constantly face is that we behave like a cost center. You may find that you have difficulty financing your projects or getting adequate participation in classes because management doesn't understand the value returned from training. It is cumbersome to calculate a return on investment that would identify, dollar for dollar, what an investment in training would return, but there are a number of other ways that you can get the organization to realize the value in training activities. The easiest is simply asking: "What would happen if we did nothing?" The cost of doing nothing can weigh heavily on an organization.

> A cost center is seen as a department that accumulates expenses or costs but doesn't contribute revenue to the organization.

Often organizations are happy when something as simple as satisfaction is improved or occurrences are reduced. They don't necessarily need to see the dollars-and-cents savings related to the training; rather, they can surmise what savings or benefits have accrued. For instance, if your organization is struggling with on-the-job injuries, you may not be able to estimate how much money a safety training program will save the company (which could include medical savings, paid sick leave, an increase in insurance premiums, and decreased productivity), but you can anticipate that the number of injuries will be reduced as a result of training, and therefore savings will be realized. Or you may find that a particular department has a higher-than-average level of turnover, and exit interviews suggest that the turnover is a direct result of the way the manager interacts with his or her employees. It may not be a worthwhile investment in time or energy to estimate the dollar savings that could be returned by lowering the turnover in that department (which would include the cost of recruiting a new worker and the time and cost factor of getting the new worker up to speed) but you can easily observe whether worker satisfaction has increased and turnover has decreased once the manager has been given management skills training and extrapolate a positive return on the investment.

Another easy way to validate the worth of training is to ask the managers requesting the training, "What would you like to see your workers doing differently at the end of the training?" If you concentrate on providing training that will hit the mark the manager has identified, then you will have proved your value to that manager. For example, a sales manager might reply, "I would like to see my salespeople bring in more quality leads. Right now, they cast a big net and reel in any ol' fish." Happily, your manager has just told you where to focus your training energies: the salespeople need to learn to qualify leads before going to the next step in the sales process. The training does not have to be extensive or complicated; it may be as simple as learning to use a ten-question checklist that gets the salesperson to consider the potential value of a customer, but so long as the outcome results in more qualified leads, you have proven your worth.

Finally, it's possible to use the success of other organizations and infer your own value from their success. If you have never designed sales training, you might consider gathering information from colleagues at other companies or professional development organizations that can give you a standardized return on investment when training is applied in this area. For instance, a quick Web search resulted in an example in the box that provides a great benchmark for sales training within an auto dealership (http://www.automax-training.com). Interestingly, it wasn't the salespeople who were being trained.

Automax, a sales training and consulting firm that serves the automotive and recreational vehicle dealership market, includes a client company case study on its Web site. The study includes a graph of month-over-month returns following the training of the dealership's service department personnel. On average, the gross profit of the service department following the training was double the amount for the same-month sales the prior year.

Budgeting for Training

There are several ways to go about creating a budget that you can defend. The method you choose might depend on what other organizations in your industry do, what data are available to you, or what your financial department dictates.

There are a number of ways that you can begin to determine the monetary needs of a training department or training initiative. Unfortunately, many of the facts and figures that you might gather will confuse you more than help you to clarify what to allot to training. Consider these statistics from the American Society for Training and Development (ASTD):

- Companies in the United States spent $54.2 billion on training in 2003.

- The mean amount spent per employee was $1,745.

- The mean percentage of payroll that companies that participated in ASTD's benchmarking forum allotted to training in 2003 was 2.05 percent.

Which of these facts (if any) correlates to your organization's financial determiners? You can choose from percentages and dollar amounts or try to figure what slice of the $54 billion belongs to you. Because there are a number of ways that training expenditures can be calculated and because it is possible that using one of these methods will assist you in determining your budgeting needs, let's take a look at the various ways to calculate a training budget request.

Resources for Locating Funding

Many federal and state government programs provide funding for work-related and job readiness training. Here are a few resources that may help you locate funding sources for your training needs:

Employment and Training Administration (ETA) Programs and Initiatives, http://www.doleta.gov/reports/program/.

For example, in May 2005, the ETA announced $125 million in grant funds for community-based job training. To apply for ETA grants, go to http://www.doleta.gov/sga/ApplyingGrants.cfm.

Employment, Labor and Training grants from Grants.gov: http://www.grants.gov/EmploymentLaborTraining.

The National Association of Workforce Boards is designed to help administer the Workforce Investment Act (via the ETA): http://www.nawb.org/.

For funding opportunities in New York State, go to http://www.workforce newyork.org/funding.htm. A little research should help you identify similar opportunities in your own state.

Percentage of Payroll

One of the easiest ways to estimate the training budget is to calculate it as a percentage of the overall payroll for your organization. Let's say your organization employs 220 employees and the average salary is $35,000, for a total of $7.7 million in yearly payroll. If you choose to allot 3 percent of payroll to training (I've picked a round number close to the low end of ASTD's benchmarked average), your total training budget would be $231,000 ($7,700,000 × .03).

> According to ASTD's 2003 benchmarking survey, annual percentages of payroll expenditures for training range from 2.34 to 8.20 percent.

Earmarking a certain percentage of payroll provides an easy-to-identify and easily understood number. However, you'll want to be sure that a percentage of payroll is the most logical way to calculate the training budget for your organization. For instance, what will happen if your company wins a new contract that will require hiring an additional seventy-five workers? If your budget is based on a percentage of payroll, it typically uses the past year's payroll as the benchmark. Now, payroll for the organization will increase in the coming year, and you will undoubtedly be responsible for a number of training initiatives associated with the new employees, neither of which has been factored into your budget request. You'll be unable to conduct the necessary training with a budget based on the historical payroll amount.

If you choose to use the percentage-of-payroll method, be sure you are aware of what changes your organization might be facing in the coming year that could require a training solution. Some changes can be predicted, and others can't; you can prepare for planned training needs based on company goals, but what about industry trends, natural disasters, or governmental rulings that might have an impact on your business and require training?

Per Head Cost

We can break down the percentage of payroll example to identify a per person cost. The $231,000 budget divided by 220 employees comes to a per head cost of $1,050. This method would be a more acceptable way to account for the additional seventy-five employees who will be hired, because training dollars are allotted on a per person basis. If your organization anticipates hiring these seventy-five employees, you can request an additional $78,750 in training budget in order to accommodate them. This method of budgeting will ensure you have training dollars allocated for each member of the company.

Benchmarking

Another way you might be able to determine how much of a training budget is necessary for your organization is to use a benchmark by determining what other organizations similar to yours allot for training. You may find this information by going to a professional association for your industry such as the National Automobile Dealers Association or the National Insurance Brokers Association, or you may choose to use a benchmark that figures how many training dollars are invested at companies of a particular size, regardless of the industry in which it operates, as Figure 3.1 illustrates.

The benefit of using a benchmark is that industry averages and historical information allow you to have a validated set of criteria, even if they do not perfectly align with your needs. One of the drawbacks to using a benchmarking methodology is that there will invariably be differences in your own organization's needs that you will want to account for, and an average doesn't offer the clarity of knowing what type of environments the benchmark companies operate in. Perhaps your industry is highly regulated and requires ongoing training that the average company would not be subject to. For example, a number of years ago, the Health Insurance Portability and Accountability Act was mandated by the U.S. federal government to ensure the confidentiality of consumers' medical data. This federal regulation required immediate training of all employees in all organizations that dealt with

FIGURE 3.1. AVERAGE TRAINING COSTS BY SIZE OF ORGANIZATION, 2004.

Source: "2004 Industry Report," *Training Magazine,* Oct. 2004.

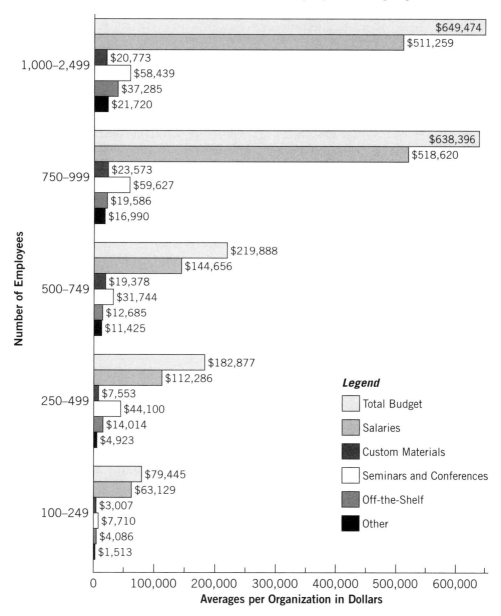

patients' medical data. This was undoubtedly a training expenditure that many organizations had not anticipated and may not have budgeted for. If you choose to use a benchmark as a starting point, be sure to consider your organization's business climate.

Another way to establish a benchmark is to poll business owners or training directors of companies that do the same type of work that your company does. If you have a local professional association, you'll be able to network with similar companies, which will give you a better indication of what companies in your same geographical area are investing in training their own workforce.

Ten Ways to Budget Better

While creating and producing a training program will always require a monetary investment, there are a number of ways in which you can save money. The following suggestions are provided by Jane Bozarth (2005), author of *e-Learning Solutions on a Shoestring: Help for the Chronically Underfunded Trainer* (for more ideas, go to www.bozarthzone.com):

1. Plan a six-month calendar. Don't think one training program at a time. Plan your training offerings at least six months in advance so that you can get better deals. For instance, facilities may give a discount on room rentals if you promise a series of rentals over the course of a few months.

2. Materials printing and reproduction. Have handouts available on the Web so that participants can download and bring with them to class.

3. Room rental. If you don't have your own training room, you can often get space below market rate at colleges and universities, especially if you hold your training in the summer when there are lots of empty rooms and free parking spaces.

4. Refreshments. Hold a training session over a brown-bag lunch so participants bring their own food. If you do provide refreshments, snacks are cheaper to provide than meals. Buy soda in large bottles rather than individual cans. Buy cups, napkins, and other paper goods in bulk.

5. Barter. Offer a course you teach for free to another business or organization in exchange for something you need. For instance, you may offer a course in time management to a college's staff in exchange for a room or to a copy shop in exchange for printing or laminating.

6. Travel. Look at whether it is cheaper to use a virtual classroom for a course versus what it would cost in travel expenses. Travel expenses add up quickly, including per diem, mileage, and the cost of people away from their desks.

7. Catalogue and create a library. Keep a library of materials you have created for your courses, such as visuals and handouts, so you don't have to recreate something you already have.

8. Use interns. High school and college students often need projects in order to earn credit. If you are located near a college, you may find students who are specializing in training, human resources, or a particular line of business who could help you.

9. Look for community resources. For instance, hospitals often provide health education, smoking cessation, and safety programs at low or no cost.

10. Use technology wisely. E-mail is free and can be used for maintaining class rosters, discussions, and pre- and posttraining assignments. Conference calls and a shared PowerPoint show can sometimes replace live meetings. And Windows users can use built-in programs such as MS Paint and MS Sound recorder to enhance presentation materials.

Summary

Having a good grasp of what training costs and, more important, what it returns promotes you and the training function as a true business partner within your organization. At the very least, you should keep track of your expenditures so that you can create a budget in the future if called on to do so. Keeping track of your expenditures will also allow you to better justify requests on an as-needed basis. Understanding the business impact and associated costs of providing training to your workforce enables both you and your organization to make sound investment decisions. Remember that it's best for the organization to train its workers and keep them.

Having a good grasp of what training needs will be necessary in the coming year will give you an idea of what you'll need to do to be prepared to tackle them. The next chapter will help you to do that.

4

Ready for the Challenge
Organization, Time and Project Management, and Technology Tools

ONE OF THE REASONS THAT I am frequently called on to assist a training department or human resource manager is not that they lack knowledge or the ability to design or develop a training program. Rather, they lack the time to get it done. After reading Chapter One, you are familiar with the many balls that you will be juggling daily. The intent of this chapter is to help you to organize these many roles and responsibilities so that you are not over-whelmed and so that you can go home each evening with a sense of accomplishment instead of a sense of trepidation about what you might have left undone. This chapter focuses on four primary topics: organization, time management, project management, and the technologies that can help you accomplish your role more efficiently and effectively.

Organization: The Key to It All

The key to being able to master the details of the role of an accidental trainer is to plan, prioritize, and schedule your daily responsibilities. One of the first things you can do to address the need for organization is to create a list of "to-do's." This will provide you with a reference so that you don't have to rely on your memory and will help you to prioritize what you do each day and week. It will also help you to determine if tasks can be combined or delegated.

Use Worksheet 4.1 to assist you in categorizing those things that you are responsible for on a monthly, weekly, or daily basis. I've started the list for you with a few suggestions that are typical responsibilities of any trainer. Don't

WORKSHEET 4.1. SAMPLE TO-DO LOG.

Monthly Responsibilities	Weekly Responsibilities	Daily Responsibilities
Expense report	Gather receipts	E-mail
Print and distribute certificates of completion	Double-check room reservations for upcoming training sessions	Return phone calls

forget the more mundane tasks like answering e-mail and returning phone calls. These are the types of tasks that can consume vast amounts of time and cause us to wonder, *Where did the day go?*

Once you have compiled a master list of responsibilities, begin to assess each column in terms of priorities and due dates. For instance, turning in expense reports may be a priority that occurs once a month; you can help to better organize yourself by making the task of gathering receipts a weekly responsibility. You can further help to organize yourself by having a special folder or envelope in which you gather any receipts that are necessary to complete your expense reports. Whenever you find a receipt in your pocket or your wallet, drop it in the envelope. This will make gathering receipts a snap when it comes time to fill out your expense reports.

Using Lists

Some lists may not look like lists at first glance. They may look more like fill-in-the-blank forms. My definition of a "list" is anything that allows me to forget about a detail or responsibility because I know it has been captured and I can refer to it later when I need it. One of my lists that gets almost daily use is a list of Web site user names and passwords. I have the list divided into categories so that it's easy to find the information I need in seconds. Some of the categories that you may want to create for your own list include subscriptions to newspapers or newsletters, professional organization member numbers, travel sites such as for airlines and hotel chains, and merchant accounts such as for training supplies or online bookstores. This computer password and user name reference list will speed your access to various sites you have subscribed to. In Worksheet 4.2, I have started the list for you, in each category, with sites that are essential to a trainer's role.

The travel confirmations checklist (Worksheet 4.3) keeps all essential travel reservation information in one place. I recommend printing it on a colored sheet of paper so that you can find it easily among your packed materials when traveling. Although I do keep each individual confirmation printout with me as well in case I need to produce them at a reservation desk, I rely solely on my travel confirmation worksheet when traveling.

WORKSHEET 4.2. PASSWORDS LOG.

Subscriptions [e-newsletters, online journals, teleconference accounts, research sites]			Associations [training-related professional associations, local chapter membership]		
Title	**User Name**	**Password**	**Association**	**User Name**	**Password**
Zoomerang			ASTD		
FreeConference			ISPI		
TrainingMag.com			SHRM		
Retail Sites [book sellers, training supply houses, printers]			Software [automatic downloads, updates]		
Retailer	**User Name**	**Password**	**Product**	**User Name**	**Password**
Amazon.com			Adobe		
Trainer's Warehouse			Microsoft		
KippBros.com					
Mimeo.com					
Travel [airline, car rental, hotel affinity programs]					
Account Name	**User Name**	**Password**			

WORKSHEET 4.3. TRAVEL CONFIRMATIONS.

Trip _____   Dates: _____–_____

AIR:

Flight Out

Airline: _____ Date: _____ Time: _____

Airport: _____ Flight #: _____

TRANSFER Airport: _____ Flight #: _____

ARRIVAL Time _____

Confirmation # _____

Notes: _____

Interim Flight

Airline: _____ Date: _____ Time: _____

Airport: _____ Flight #: _____

TRANSFER Airport: _____ Flight #: _____

ARRIVAL Time _____

Confirmation # _____

Notes: _____

Return Flight

Airline: _____ Date: _____ Time: _____

Airport: _____ Flight #: _____

TRANSFER Airport: _____ Flight #: _____

ARRIVAL Time _____

Confirmation # _____

Notes: _____

HOTEL:

Name: _____ Address: _____

Phone: (___)_____ Dates: _____–_____

Room Type: ☐ Double ☐ King ☐ Suite Rate: _____ Confirmation # _____

Notes: _____

CAR:

Agency: _____ Dates: _____–_____ Type car: _____

Confirm # _____ Rate: _____ per _____ Estimated Total: _____

Notes: _____

_____

_____

_____

Lists and worksheets capture everything that requires your attention and gives you the peace of mind of knowing where to find it again when it's time to apply that information. They also enable you to delegate duties by handing them off to assistants or vendors (such as hotels or caterers), because they'll have all the details they need to get a job done. An alternative to using lists is to create a journal using a spiral-bound notebook. In it you will make a note of each item you must attend to, with a time estimate and a due date if applicable. As items are accomplished, you can check them off or cross them out. A benefit of this method is that you have an ongoing list of to-do's and accomplishments in one handy reference.

Creating Templates

Nothing wastes more time and energy than recreating the wheel. Rather than thinking about creating materials for your marketing, announcements, and invitations or for classroom materials, think about creating templates. A template allows you to put your creative energies into the piece just once and then use it as the basis for all similar future pieces. Some items you will need on a daily basis that lend themselves easily to template creation include:

- Announcements of training courses (e-mail or print)
- Training registration confirmations
- Class rosters
- Directions to off-site training facilities
- Evaluation forms
- Certificates of completion
- Requests for proposals from vendors

Finally, one of the keys to good organization is to constantly reassess your practices. At the end of each day, check your to-do list to ensure that priority items have been addressed and lesser priority items have been moved to another list or another day. On a weekly basis, look back through your journal to make sure you are still aware of what needs to be done (and to cross off those things you've accomplished).

Managing Your Time Effectively

You will never find time for anything. If you want it, you must make it.
—Charles Buxton

Because you are either a one-person department or fitting training in among your other duties, your time will be at a premium. With a little organization, forethought, and standards that define where and when you'll spend your time, you will be able to maximize the limited number of hours you have each day for designing, developing, or coordinating training. For instance, what would you do with your time if I told you that beginning now, you have thirty free minutes with absolutely nothing scheduled? If you were to offer me that same thirty minutes, it would take me just a moment to identify three or four tasks that I could complete, such as filing, returning a few phone calls, or proofreading.

Taking Control of Time

When you understand where your time is spent, and perhaps more important, where your time is best used, you will be in the position to control it. I believe controlling your time and managing your time are different. When you have control of your time, you define when and for what purpose your time is used and avoid allowing others to define it for you. Managing your time involves maximizing the limited amount of hours available to you.

One of my favorite control techniques is to just say no. Let's assume a departmental manager comes to you with a request for training; saying no can be as simple as, "That sounds like a great initiative, but I'm afraid our training calendar is maxed out for the next quarter. Would you like to implement it later this year?" Saying no allows you to set and protect boundaries. Of course it's easier when you have an understanding of what your responsibilities are at any given time. If you didn't know that your training schedule was completely full for the next few months, you might be tempted to accommodate the manager's request. But what if the request for additional training came from your boss? How do you say no to your boss? An effective technique is to have him or her make the decision. Say, "Here are the seven initiatives that I am focused on at the moment. Which one of these do you want to stop working on so that I can address this new priority?" This control technique allows you to maintain your boundaries by replacing one initiative with another rather than taking on additional work.

One of the more successful ways to control your time is to develop standards that will define how you use it. You may want to start by keeping track of how you now spend your time. It is difficult to know where you are "wasting" time and might regain it if you don't know where you spend it in the first place. Although this exercise is time-consuming, I believe you will gain valuable insight about the way you manage time, and you'll need to conduct the exercise only once to gain years of benefit from the insight. All you need is a legal pad numbered in fifteen-minute increments, beginning at the time you start your day and ending at the time you go home.

Every fifteen minutes, pause for a moment to jot down what you are doing at that moment: checking e-mail, taking a phone call, designing a training program, or something else. Don't stop to analyze how to spend your week until the week is complete. At the end of the week, take twenty to thirty minutes to review your time log and look for patterns. This might be easier if you color-code your activities—for instance, highlighting phone calls in yellow, meetings in blue, e-mails in green, and the time spent in designing, developing, or delivering training, highlighted in a fourth color.

Once you have completed this analysis, you can start to develop best practices for using time more effectively. Assessing your time so that you can control it enables you to consistently work toward your training goals rather than allowing others to define your time and activities for you. There are a number of best practices suggested in the next section, which will help you to get started.

Tips and Tools for Time Management

Earlier in this chapter I discussed knowing what your commitments and responsibilities are in order to know if you are capable of taking on more. One of the ways that you can easily reference your commitments is by using a two- or three-month wall calendar. Use different colored markers to denote different training initiatives, such as green for a finance course for nonfinancial managers and red for a course for customer service skills. The use of multiple colors will help you quickly recognize commitments by topic or department. The wall calendar will also help others to visualize your responsibilities, which helps when you must say no.

Sorting E-Mail. Setting up folders within your e-mail system allows you to sort and organized incoming messages. The most important e-mail folder you can create is a junk folder. I look in my junk folder at the beginning and end of each day to ensure that messages I want to receive have not accidentally been routed there. Once I'm sure that all of the messages contained in the junk mail folder are indeed junk, I empty the folder.

Having messages organized allows you to prioritize your response to them. You may want to set up folders for individuals, departments, or vendors you deal with on a regular basis. For example, each of my clients has a folder in my e-mail system. When a message comes in from their domain name, it is automatically routed to the appropriate folder. In this way, I don't lose important messages among the rest of my e-mail. I can also quickly look in the folder to see if the message is something I need to respond to or if it's simply information the client has sent me to assist in my work. E-mail management enables me to answer priority e-mails in a timely way and to spend no more than five minutes of my day dealing with junk mail.

Communicating Expectations. Have you ever gone to a restaurant and been told that there is a thirty-minute wait for a table? When the hostess calls you in twenty minutes, you're elated. The reason is that the hostess communicated an expectation and then exceeded it. A number of time management issues can be addressed in a similar manner. For instance, how simple would it be to relieve the stress of twelve messages in your voice mailbox by simply leaving an outgoing message for callers: "I will be off-site conducting training classes Monday through Friday this week and will do my best to return your call before the end of the week." This communicates the expectation to your callers that they will not receive a timely callback and relieves you of the stress of trying to figure out how to check messages and return calls in the middle of a training session. An out-of-office message sent in response to e-mails will communicate to others that you will respond to them when your schedule allows.

Using Block Time and Burst Time. We have all blocks and bursts of time available to us; time management is achieved by understanding what we can accomplish during these periods of time. Blocks of time may be one, two, or three hours. They are useful for meetings, interviews, research, writing, reviewing, and the design of training programs. Bursts of time come in ten-, twenty-, or thirty-minute increments. They are good for checking e-mail and voice mail, returning or placing calls, sorting through mail, perusing catalogues, and filing. The effective use of bursts of time requires lists. If you keep a master list of small but necessary tasks on your desk, you will be able to accomplish much more each day. When you suddenly find yourself with ten minutes to spare before you must join a conference call, you can quickly skim the list to see what might be possible to accomplish in ten minutes.

> **TIP** Organization and time management expert Anita Taylor suggests, "If something will take less than two minutes to accomplish—just do it!" (personal communication).

Trash, Act, or Delegate (T.A.D.). When handling things such as mail, e-mail, and voice mail messages, be ruthless about what your next action should be. If the item has no further purpose, *trash* it. If the item is something you should *act* on, then do so. And finally, be ruthless about what it is that you personally need to take care of. Whenever possible, *delegate* to someone else. For instance, in order to be able to write this book, I needed to clear time on my schedule. I took a hard look at what I was doing on a daily and weekly basis and was able to identify a number of things that I could ask others to do. By delegating these tasks, my role became more of an overseer, which freed up about two hours in my schedule each day. Make sure everything on your to-do list is a good use of your time. If it is not, give it to someone else. You may be thinking to yourself, *I'm a one-person department! There's nobody to delegate to!* Don't fret. Here are a few ways that you can delegate to others without having a staff:

- Hire a temporary worker. It may be essential that PowerPoint slides be created for your upcoming training course, but is it essential that you personally create them? If there's no one else in the company you can delegate this task to, find a short-term worker from a temporary agency with the skills that you need. Make sure you check with your HR department, which probably has a service it regularly uses.
- Hire an intern from a local college or high school. An intern can proofread, file, copy and collate, collect training evaluations, and write first drafts of reports for you. An intern is a wonderful choice because this is a person you will have on a regular basis and to whom you can assign ongoing duties. Frequently interns need work experience to gain credit and aren't allowed to be paid.
- Consider other employees within your own organization who might like to expand their knowledge and skills. When I was a one-person department, I was blessed with a coworker from the sales department who wanted to learn more about training and development. She worked out an arrangement with her boss to spend four hours a week in my department.
- Delegate to independent contractors, freelancers, and vendors (see Chapter Six for more information in this area). This method is the most costly option, so consider the need for outside resources at the start of a project in case you need to request appropriate funding.

We all have the same amount of time available to us each day. Understanding and mastering how you use your time—through the implementation of systems, communicating expectations, or prioritizing and delegating—is key to managing your day-to-day responsibilities. But often you'll find yourself managing a project, the topic of the next section.

Managing Projects

Project management is a term that can strike fear in the hearts of most people. Saying the words "Project Management" usually suggests terms such as PERT, GANTT, and critical path. While these technical terms are true project management functions, I'm happy to tell you that we will not be dealing with the technical side of project management in this section (although I do recommend taking a project management course to enhance your own professional skills). Half the battle in successfully managing a project is being organized and using your time efficiently, the two topics we've already covered in this chapter. In addition, successful project management requires advance planning and being able to respond nimbly when things don't go as planned.

Project Planning

Planning is essential to the timely accomplishment of any project. Having a plan that breaks down a project into smaller tasks and to-do items allows you to continually make progress without feeling overwhelmed. Planning is also crucial because once the project is up and running, it can be expensive in both time and money to discover that you have missed a key task. Imagine scheduling a training course but forgetting to reserve a room in which to conduct it.

Planning is easier when you have a methodology to follow. Worksheet 4.4 is one way to organize the various details involved in planning and managing a project, such as tasks, people, and deliverables. You may find it easier to create a plan that is organized more like a diagram, as in Figure 4.1, or perhaps create a plan that mimics a storyboard using sticky notes that allow you to color-code tasks and subtasks and move them around as necessary.

FIGURE 4.1. TRAINING DESIGN.

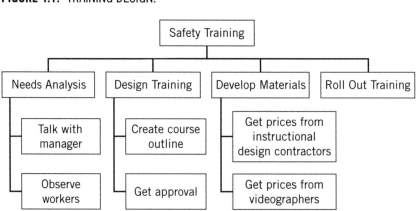

WORKSHEET 4.4. PLANNING WORKSHEET.

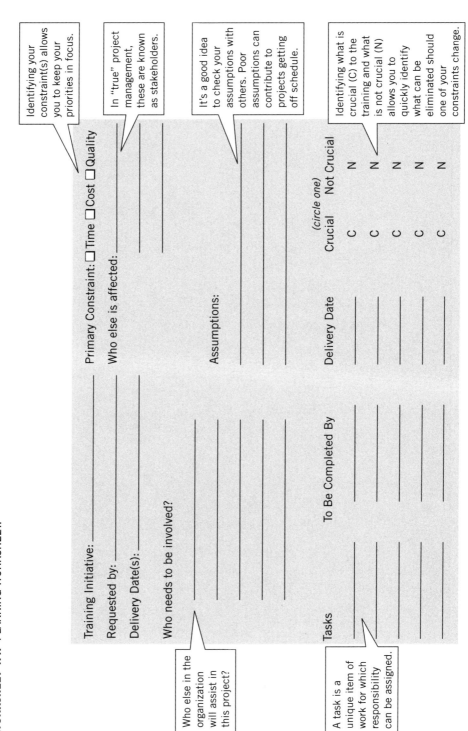

Training Initiative: _____

Requested by: _____

Delivery Date(s): _____

Primary Constraint: ☐ Time ☐ Cost ☐ Quality

Who else is affected: _____

Identifying your constraint(s) allows you to keep your priorities in focus.

In "true" project management, these are known as stakeholders.

Who needs to be involved?

_____

_____

_____

Who else in the organization will assist in this project?

Assumptions:

_____

_____

_____

It's a good idea to check your assumptions with others. Poor assumptions can contribute to projects getting off schedule.

Tasks	To Be Completed By	Delivery Date	(circle one)	
			Crucial	Not Crucial
_____	_____	_____	C	N
_____	_____	_____	C	N
_____	_____	_____	C	N
_____	_____	_____	C	N
_____	_____	_____	C	N

A task is a unique item of work for which responsibility can be assigned.

Identifying what is crucial (C) to the training and what is not crucial (N) allows you to quickly identify what can be eliminated should one of your constraints change.

(continued)

WORKSHEET 4.4. PLANNING WORKSHEET *(continued)*.

Task

Transfer your tasks from the list above here.

Subtasks

Most tasks need to be broken down into more manageable subtasks.

If you keep your project planning worksheet on a computer, you can easily move the tasks and subtasks into the order in which they should be done.

Equipment/Supplies

-
-
-
-
-

Costs

$ _____
$ _____
$ _____
$ _____
$ _____

You may need to purchase equipment or supplies such as videos or calculators.

On a weekly basis, review the planning worksheet and make any necessary changes. Perhaps you will need to add a task or ask for assistance from someone within the organization. You may choose to print or copy the project plan each week and highlight those things you intend to accomplish in the coming week. This method will allow you to see what tasks can be done simultaneously or in parallel with other tasks.

You can use the worksheet for more than planning. For example, you can use it to track the length of time tasks take to accomplish and the costs that the project has incurred. This type of tracking will enable you to plan future projects more easily and accurately and also make reporting easier if you must give regular updates to upper management or internal clients. Planning gives you control over your projects and allows you to easily visualize and measure your progress.

Responding to Issues or Changes in Plan

Rarely does any project go according to plan. One of the benefits of creating a project plan is the ability to see the project both as a whole and in its components, which allows you to identify areas of flexibility should a change to the plan be required. Here are some examples of changes in plan that needed to be accommodated as a training project progressed:

• An online survey was distributed to the managers of workers who were scheduled for two days of professional development. The survey offered a number of potential topics to be covered during the training and asked the managers to rank-order their perceived need for each topic. No one responded to the survey.

• A full-day training program was designed for salespeople at the request of their managers. Approximately a week before the training delivery date, word was received that the "big boss" wanted one hour to address the salespeople after lunch, since it was rare for all of the salespeople to be together.

• A self-study training program—PowerPoint with audio—was designed for retail locations across the United States. During the design phase, it was determined that approximately half of the computers at the retail locations did not include sound cards and speakers.

Being responsive to changes in the project plan may require you to answer such issues as these:

- *Where can I make up time if we get off schedule?* For example, rather than creating structured role plays, have participants submit a list of their toughest challenges that will be discussed in class. This approach could save you a day or more of design time.

- *Can a process be eliminated?* You could e-mail the workbook to participants and ask them to print it and bring it with them rather than printing and binding the workbooks yourself.

- *Is it possible to combine one step with another, or is it possible to unbundle steps?* Can you conduct interviews with managers while they are gathered together for another meeting rather than conducting one-on-one interviews with them in their own offices?

- *What will happen if part of the process is not completed until after the training has begun to roll out?* One training project that required homework between sessions got off schedule, and there was not enough time to create the homework for inclusion in the classroom materials. Since the trainees didn't need the homework until the end of the training class, it was developed while the participants attended the training, and handed out before they left. The rollout schedule was not affected, although working down to the wire certainly was not the original plan for the completion of materials.

Having a well-thought-out project plan is the first step to successful implementation. Armed with the plan, you can request appropriate resources, provide useful updates to project sponsors, and quickly see when you may be in danger of missing a deliverable.

Technology Solutions

While it's true that some things in our lives have gotten more complicated with the advent of technology, it's also true that we can accomplish more and be better organized through the use of certain technologies. Try some of these technological tools for yourself to make your life a little easier.

Survey Tools

Survey tools allow you to gather information quickly from managers, employees, or people outside your organization who might assist you in the creation of training programs. Two free online survey tools are available from www. Zoomerang.com and www.SurveyMonkey.com. Both services are Web based and allow you to enter your survey online and send it to survey participants using a Web link. The free offerings of these two services do limit what you are allowed to do, such as the number of questions you can ask, but overall either one will serve your needs and you'll be able to have a professional survey sent out to all of the managers in your company within twenty minutes. Each service also offers fee-based subscription services that provide more options, such as branding your survey with your own company logo or downloading survey results to your own computer.

Research Tools

The Internet is a wonderful research tool, but the results can be overwhelming. Try www.Pluck.com, an add-on to your existing browser. Pluck allows you to conduct searches of the Internet and newswires by key word or phrase and retrieve the results in one window and view them in another; you never have to navigate away from your browser page in order to view search results. Pluck also allows you to create "perches," which are ongoing searches. A perch will "troll" the Internet for you, even when your browser is not running, and continue to retrieve new results that meet your perch criteria. The new results will be added to your perch folder for viewing at your convenience.

Google offers a number of specialty searches that can help you target your Internet searches. Try these:

- http://www.images.google.com to find photos and clip art for inclusion in your training materials

- http://www.news.google.com for up-to-date news stories that may affect your topic

- http://www.scholar.google.com for references associated with academic papers and research

You can also use Define:word in the Google search field (such as "Define:cost center"), when you need the official definition of a word or term.

Printing and Reproduction

The administrative tasks of having materials printed or copied and bound can take hours out of your day and aren't a good use of your time. The following services allow you to work right up to the last moment and still have professional materials ready for your training sessions:

• Mimeo (http://www.Mimeo.com) or FedEx Kinkos will print and bind materials from your own files. Each service will deliver to your door (or a remote training location) by the next day as long as your order is received in time, which is usually well after what you might consider regular business hours.

• Quantum Copy (http://www.QuantumCopy.com) and VistaPrint (http://www.VistaPrint.com) allow you to create colorful, graphically designed materials with their easy-to-navigate, on-line templates.

Instructional Design Software

Much like printing and reproduction, the creation of training materials can take a good deal of time. The following instructional design software packages help to create professional materials with minimal effort:

• Langevin Instructional DesignWare, http://www.Langevin.com

• LeaderGuide Pro by Great Circle Learning, http://www.GCLearning.com

• Designer's Edge by Allen Communication Learning Services, http://www.allencomm.com

Miscellaneous Tools

Each of these tools will assist you in better organizing your roles and responsibilities:

• On Project, http:// www.onproject.com, a Web-based project management service that allows you to manage multiple projects, deliverables, and the input from many contributors. Affordable monthly subscription fee.

- Computer-based Stickies that stay on your computer desktop. Freeware available from http://www.zhornsoftware.co.uk.

- Dragon Naturally Speaking, IBM ViaVoice, or iListen (Macintosh). Voice dictation software takes an hour or two to acclimate to your voice but can save you hundreds of future hours by allowing you to dictate your training materials, e-mail, instant messages, and more. (That's how this book was written.)

- Microsoft OneNote 2003, http://www.microsoft.com/office/onenote/, which allows you to make lists and keep notes in various folders that you set up the way you want them to work.

- You Send It, a Web-based site that allows you to send large files that are too big to transmit using regular e-mail. Great for sending files to yourself at home. Free from http://www.YouSendIt.com.

Summary

It takes a lot to be successful: preparation, planning, time management, and technology. But most of all, it takes discipline. Experiment with the suggestions in this chapter and decide which tools and techniques work for you; then commit yourself to implementing them. It will be well worth the effort when you are known throughout the organization for producing great training, the subject of the next chapter.

Producing Training Programs

Y OU'VE UNDOUBTEDLY ATTENDED many training programs in your career, so you have a good idea of what it is like to be a participant. As superficial as it may sound, a large part of a successful training is its production value. Before your trainees even become involved in the content of the course, they will make judgments about the value of your program based on the environment in which the training is conducted. The most common location for training is in a classroom, that is, everyone comes to a common room with an instructor. There are other options for training, however, so this chapter starts with an overview of the different ways that training can be delivered. This will provide you with a menu of options from which to choose when you are determining the best delivery method for a particular topic or a particular audience. Since more than 70 percent of all workplace training is classroom based, either on-site or off-site, the remainder of the chapter focuses on the myriad of details required to organize and produce a successful training program.

Training Programs Defined

Training can be delivered in a number of ways. A training program can be a full day, a half-day, or multiple days of instruction. It might be held on-site at your facility or off-site at a hotel or conference center. Training may also include self-study work, which a trainee conducts on his or her own, or with the guidance of a coach as the individual's schedule allows. Training is also accomplished through conference calls, webinars, and videoconferencing. The method of delivery is typically chosen so that it complements the topics being taught—for example:

- A lecture is typically a presentation or demonstration by one or more speakers. It employs a minimal amount of participant interaction, usually in the form of a question-and-answer session at the end of the presentation. Lectures work best when they are interspersed throughout a workshop because most people cannot concentrate on a lecture for more than twenty minutes.

- A workshop engages participants in exercises, case studies, or other hands-on activities. The emphasis is on group interaction.

- Roundtables are used for group discussions, brainstorming, or problem solving in small groups. This format is beneficial if participants will gain value by interacting with their peers.

- A cracker barrel presentation features a number of guest speakers seated at various stations throughout the training room and has the participants rotate among the stations and experts.

- Conference calls are useful for short presentations that require no audio-visual support or participant interaction and when the training group is geographically dispersed.

- Web conferences and videoconferences are useful when it is important to have the participants interact with one another but it is not crucial that they be in the same location.

- A retreat is typically a two- or three-day event held at a getaway location such as a resort or mountain cabin. Retreats are used when the participants need to be intensely focused on the topic at hand.

- Self-study training is an independent activity for the learner that may be in the form of reading or a tutorial accessed using the Internet or a CD or DVD.

The remainder of this chapter is arranged around the training program planning guide in Worksheet 5.1, which covers most of what you will need to consider or attend to in order to produce a classroom-based training program that is appropriate for and well received by your audience.

WORKSHEET 5.1. TRAINING PROGRAM PLANNING GUIDE.

Title: _____ # of attendees _____ Facilities ☐ on-site ☐ off-site

Location: _____

Name: _____

Phone: _____

Room arrangement: ☐ Classroom ☐ U-shape ☐ Rounds ☐ Crescent ☐ Chevron ☐ Theater

Breakout Rooms needed: ☐ Yes ☐ No If yes, # _____

Dates: ☐ Mon ☐ Tues ☐ Wed ☐ Thur ☐ Fri ☐ Sat ☐ Sun

Times: A.M. __/__ __/__ __/__ __/__ __/__ __/__ __/__

P.M.

A/V required:

Days required: ☐ Flip charts # _____ ☐ LCD projector ☐ Overhead projector ☐ Screen ☐ TV/VCR/DVD

Materials: ☐ Trainer's Tool Kit ☐ Transparencies ☐ Handout #1

☐ Leader Guide # _____ ☐ PowerPoint file (& backup) ☐ Handout #2

☐ Workbooks # _____ ☐ Name tents/tags # _____ ☐ Handout #3

☐ blank ☐ pre-printed

Purchased materials: _____ Date: _____ Vendor: _____

Reproduction: ☐ in-house ☐ outsourced Vendor: _____

☐ pick up ☐ to be delivered date _____ to whose attention _____ where _____

Food and beverage: # _____

☐ Mon ☐ Tues ☐ Wed ☐ Thur ☐ Fri ☐ Sat ☐ Sun

A.M. break ___ ___ ___ ___ ___ ___ ___

P.M. break ___ ___ ___ ___ ___ ___ ___

Lunch time ___ ___ ___ ___ ___ ___ ___

☐ on-own, outside facility ☐ on-own, at facility ☐ catered ☐ facility provides

☐ working lunch ☐ separate room

Special needs? ☐ allergy ☐ vegetarian ☐ diet restrictions (list) _____

Notes:

Choosing the Location

The environment, whether large or small, formal or informal, helps set the appropriate tone for the training. When thinking about the right location, consider the objectives of the training, the length of the course, and, naturally, your budget. Decide whether it might be appropriate or necessary to hold the meeting off-site. For example, sometimes a neutral off-site location is necessary for confidential information or for the comfort of senior-level management and executives who may be in attendance. The following options present the four primary locations for training programs.

On-Site Meeting Space

On-site training space is often the best option. It can be arranged quickly and easily and, above all, is cost-effective. In addition, you'll have most reference material readily available. Unless employees from other office locations are expected to attend, you won't have to worry about travel time or expenses. An office, boardroom, or small conference room works well if you do not have dedicated training space. Take steps to prevent distractions like ringing telephones or employee interruptions. A "Training in Progress" sign on the door works wonders to keep distractions to a minimum.

Local Off-Site Meeting Space

Getting away from the office environment can stimulate creativity and generally makes a nice change from the often mundane day-to-day office surroundings. This is a good option when privacy is needed, perhaps for sensitive training issues. When selecting an off-site location, whether you're looking for a local hotel conference room, a restaurant, or other meeting space, your budget will dictate your options. To be safe, always inspect the space in person before making a final decision. Make sure the space is the right size for the group you will be hosting.

Out-of-Town, On-Site Meeting Space

This option applies only if your company has offices in other locations. These kinds of training meetings often take place when another facility has something, such as new equipment, that employees at your facility need to see. If possible, visit the site beforehand to set up any necessary details. Alternatively, if you have a counterpart at the facility, coordinate with that person to make all the arrangements. Consider travel and accommodations as possible additional expenses for your attendees.

Out-of-Town, Off-Site Meeting Space

This option is usually reserved for training programs that need to pack a special punch because costs will inevitably be much higher. These kinds of programs may last several days; consider using a resort facility that offers enjoyable relaxation options such as golfing, swimming, or a fitness center. A site visit is essential.

For off-site meeting space, ask the facility about its insurance policy. For example, find out who is responsible if one of your participants slips and hurts herself.

Source: Adapted from Friedmann, S. *Meetings and Event Planning for Dummies.* Hoboken, N.J.: Wiley, 2003. Reprinted with permission from John Wiley & Sons, Inc.

Choosing the Location

Choosing a training location can have far-reaching implications such as what time training can start, how many people can be accommodated, and what types of activities can be successfully conducted within the space. The top of the Training Program Planning Guide (Figure 5.1) acts as a reference for you by detailing the name of the program, the number of attendees you expect, and the location of the training session.

FIGURE 5.1.

Training Program Planning Guide

Title: Intro to Supervision   # of Attendees 12   Facilities ☐ on-site ☒ off-site

Location: Hilton-downtown

Name: Rachel Jones

Phone: 888-282-4165 x102

An on-site location might be a dedicated training room or a borrowed conference room at your office location. In the example in Figure 5.1, the location is given as the Hilton-downtown, but it could just as easily say "Conference Room B, 3rd floor." If your training will be located off-site, the location may be a company facility other than the one where you work (such as the corporate office or a satellite facility), or it may be a rented facility such as a hotel or conference center. When conducting your training at an off-site facility, always be sure to have a contact person's name and phone number. Even when the off-site facility is owned by your company, it is helpful to have someone at that location who can assist you when you discover that your training room is locked or that your handouts have not arrived and you need copies made.

> **TIP** Hotels typically charge separately for each requirement, such as room rental, audiovisual rental, and refreshments. Conference facilities typically charge a per head fee that includes everything required.

Room Characteristics to Consider

When choosing the appropriate space for your training, whether in your own office or at an off-site location, pay attention to the characteristics of the room or rooms you are considering:

- *Space.* Will everyone be able to fit comfortably into the room after you have set up chairs, tables, aisles, and any audiovisual equipment that is needed?
- *Temperature.* Does the room have air-conditioning or heating? Can you control the temperature during the meeting in case body heat causes the temperature to rise uncomfortably? Unfortunately, windows aren't a good substitute for air-conditioning because they let in outside noises and distractions along with fresh air.

• *Lighting.* How much control do you have over the room lighting? Can you make the room dark enough for the audience to see images projected on a screen? Can you make it light enough for participants to take notes?

• *Sight lines.* Will you be unable to seat participants in any areas of the room because of a column, low ceiling, or other obstruction?

• *Potential distractions.* What potential distractions might make the room less than ideal as a training room? Is the air-conditioner too loud? Is there noise from a busy street? Does foot traffic echo in the hallway outside? Is the room adjacent to a kitchen or near another training room where an audio system might be in use?

• *Seating and tables.* Does the meeting room include tables and chairs, or will you have to rent them? Does the facility charge a separate fee for room setup? Are you required to rent from the facility, or can you use an outside provider?

• *Rental time.* Be sure you have access to the room early enough to set up and troubleshoot any unanticipated problems before the training class begins. Allow time for audiovisual technicians, lighting technicians, food service providers, and any other vendors that need access to the room before participants arrive.

• *Essential items.* Find out in advance whether the facility provides the following essential items free or for an additional fee:

- Coverings for tables such as tablecloths or table skirts

- Water and glasses for participants

- Notepads and pencils

- A lectern, if appropriate

- Easels or signed holders to direct participants to the proper room

- Extension cords, power strips, and extra tables for your projection equipment

- Audiovisual equipment such as a projector, screen, flip charts, and easels

Source: Adapted from Friedmann, S. *Meetings and Event Planning for Dummies.* Hoboken, N.J.: Wiley, 2003. Reprinted with permission from John Wiley & Sons, Inc.

Noting the number of attendees expected for the training class will assist you in a number of ways. It will help you to:

- Determine an appropriate room setup (discussed in the next section).

- Determine how many deliveries of the course should be offered. For example, a workshop-type training session is most successful with twenty or fewer participants. If you have one hundred participants to train, you will need to offer the same training session five different times.

- Ascertain the appropriate number of classroom materials or refreshments to order.

On-site or off-site decisions are primarily dictated by money: if you have no discretionary funds, you'll be forced to conduct your training at your location or another company-owned facility. On-site trainings run the risk of constant interruption, however, because your participants may be called away to attend to matters related to their work. If you think there is a potential that your attendees will be called away (or will not return from breaks), you may want to get them away from the workplace at an off-site location, which will minimize their distractions. Equally as important as an appropriate location, the arrangement of the room can have an impact on the success of your program as well.

Room Arrangement

Seating arrangements are crucial to creating an environment in which participants are able to interact with one another and gain the most from the training session (Figure 5.2). The purpose of the training and the size of the audience

FIGURE 5.2.

Room Arrangement: ☐ Classroom ☒ U-shape ☐ Rounds ☐ Crescent ☐ Chevron ☐ Theater
Breakout Rooms Needed: ☐ Yes ☒ No   If yes, # _____

should be considered when determining the appropriate room arrangement. For instance, a training session on team building would be enhanced by a seating arrangement that groups the participants in twos or fours. Pharmaceutical companies tend to conduct new product training for their salespeople in large groups of a hundred or more; the most appropriate seating arrangement for that type of training is theater or auditorium style. The most common options and an explanation of when they are best used are in Figure 5.3.

FIGURE 5.3. OPTIONS FOR ROOM ARRANGEMENTS.

Classroom   Classroom-style seating includes a table at which two or three participants can sit comfortably. This seating arrangement works best when the participants need a workspace to take notes or participate in activities.

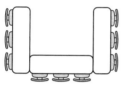

U-Shape   The **U**-shape or horseshoe-shape seating arrangement seats participants around the outer edges of the **U**. This allows all participants to see one another and allows the instructor to move in closer to the group (by using the center of the **U**) rather than being limited to the front of the room.

Rounds   Rounds can accommodate six to eight participants and work best when the focus of the training is on participant interaction, such as team building or problem solving. A disadvantage is that some participants will have their backs to the instructor. Rounds also take up quite a bit of physical space; more tables will be required to accommodate the same number of participants as you can accommodate in the classroom or **U**-shape arrangements.

(continued)

FIGURE 5.3. OPTIONS FOR ROOM ARRANGEMENTS *(continued).*

Crescent   The crescent arrangement is similar to rounds; however, participants are seated on only one side of the table. This seating arrangement has the benefits associated with round seating but allows all participants to have a visual connection with the instructor at the front of the room. The space disadvantage of rounds is exacerbated when using crescent seating because of the limited number of participants at each table.

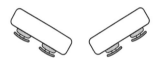

Chevron   The chevron design, a variation of classroom-style seating, uses the same tables and the same number of participants per table, but the arrangement of the tables lends itself to more visual contact among participants, which encourages better interaction.

Theater   Theater-style seating arranges participants in rows facing the speaker. This is common for large groups. This style of seating is least conducive to note taking and participant interaction. It is best used when the training objective is simply a transmission of information.

Sometimes other rooms are needed in addition to the main classroom; these breakout rooms are often used if the training design incorporates small group work. When participants are sent off during the class session to collaborate in small groups, they frequently go to their own breakout rooms. The use of breakout rooms can be effective, but they are typically not practical for a number of reasons. It is usually difficult to locate a number of empty offices or conference rooms at your own workplace, and if your training is being held at a hotel or conference center, there will be additional rental fees. Also, since breakout rooms are used only for small group work, they will probably be idle for a good portion of your training program. If the idea of breakout rooms is appealing but the drawbacks are not, the same type of group interaction can be achieved by sending small groups to work in the four corners of the training room or sending the groups to work in the lobby or an outdoor seating area.

Dates and Times

The dates and times portion of the Training Program Planning Guide (Figure 5.4) has space for a seven-day schedule, broken into A.M. and P.M. segments in order to accommodate a variety of options. For instance, some training sessions begin in the evening with a cocktail reception or dinner for the participants and presenters prior to the first day of training. Or a multiday program may begin at 1:00 P.M. the first day to allow participants to travel in the morning, and then continue for a full day on the second day. Weekend dates are included on the checklist to accommodate training programs that require participants to arrive the night before training starts or stay the day after training is over. After-hours and weekend accommodations are typical when a training program is being held off-site or the training is intended to be a retreat. Specifically noting the days, dates, and times of the training program helps to alleviate any confusion about arrival or departure times, or the times during which the training will be conducted.

FIGURE 5.4.

Dates:	☐ Mon	☒ Tues	☒ Wed	☐ Thur	☐ Fri	☐ Sat	☐ Sun
		4/20	4/21				
Times: A.M.	___ – ___	8:30 – ___	8:30 – ___	___ – ___	___ – ___	___ – ___	___ – ___
P.M.	___ – ___	– 5:00	– 5:00	___ – ___	___ – ___	___ – ___	___ – ___

Audiovisual Requirements

Every training program requires some form of audiovisual (A/V) equipment. The most typical pieces are listed on the planning guide (Figure 5.5) and include flip charts, PowerPoint slides, and electronics (overhead projectors, LCD projectors, microphones). Depending on your resources and where the training will be conducted, you may need to rent audiovisual equipment; off-site facilities rarely allow you to bring your own. Flip charts are extremely useful for the instructor to use to capture group brainstorming ideas and by the participants when working in small groups. A training facility such as a hotel or conference center will charge for each flip chart pad you require.

FIGURE 5.5.

One of the easiest formats to create training presentations in is Microsoft's PowerPoint. PowerPoint will allow you to print your slides as transparencies to use with an overhead projector or display the file directly from your computer using an LCD projector. An advantage of LCD projectors is that they can be used to show anything that can be accessed from the computer, including PowerPoint slides, Web pages, and software.

Which type of equipment you choose to use may in part be dictated by your budget. An overhead projector is more economical, but it's also becoming archaic technology and is rather cumbersome to transport. An LCD projector is much more compact but also more expensive. You may be able to offset the cost of an LCD projector by sharing the cost with other departments that also make presentations, such as the sales department. Projecting anything (transparencies or computer images) often requires a screen unless the training room has a large blank wall that can be used in place of a screen.

Audiovisual Equipment for Training Programs

Here is a list of audiovisual equipment most commonly used for training programs:

- *LCD.* The most current piece of equipment these days is a laptop computer that uses an LCD projector to project images onto a screen. Because LCD projectors rent for about five hundred dollars a day, you may want to consider purchasing one if you are going to use it regularly.
- *VCR or DVD.* A TV/VCR or DVD combination enables the trainer to show training videos related to the presentation. Make sure that you know how to operate the equipment and that the video is set to play at the starting point, so all that needs to be done is to hit the Play button.
- *Overhead projector.* Many trainers still feel comfortable using an overhead projector. Make sure to have plenty of transparencies and transparency markers on hand, preferably in black or blue. These colors have the most impact when projected onto a screen. Red is best for underlining major points, but avoid a red/green combination because color-blind individuals will see those colors as gray. Also, orange and yellow will wash out when projected onto a screen.
- *Flip chart.* Flip charts are particularly good for capturing ideas and brainstorming sessions and can be posted on the walls of the training room for reference. Be sure to have plenty of pads and markers available. Black and blue are the best colors to use because they are easy to read from a distance.
- *Microphone.* Depending on the size of the group and the training space, you may need a microphone system. Among the choices are a stationary microphone attached to a podium or lectern, a hand-held microphone (beware the long cord!), or a lavaliere or wireless microphone.

Source: Adapted from Friedmann, S. *Meetings and Event Planning for Dummies.* Hoboken, N.J.: Wiley, 2003. Reprinted with permission from John Wiley & Sons, Inc.

You may require a TV and VCR or DVD player in order to conduct a portion of the training; this is especially true of training programs that are purchased off-the-shelf and frequently come packaged with an A/V component. Off-site facilities typically charge for audiovisual equipment on a daily basis. You can save money by renting the equipment for just one day rather than for the duration of the training program. Depending on the purpose of the training and the size of the audience, you may also require a sound system or staging. So far the Training Program Planning Guide has addressed arrangements that create the right atmosphere and ensure a successful learning environment. The remainder of the worksheet addresses more participant-oriented requirements.

Materials and Reproduction

The materials and reproduction sections of the Training Program Planning Guide (Figure 5.6) will ensure that you have all the materials necessary to conduct a training class. The Trainer's Tool Kit includes markers, masking tape, and other accessories that a trainer may need during a training class (see Chapter One for a complete list of items to keep in your tool kit). Depending on how many instructors will be teaching, a leader guide will be required for each, and visual media such as PowerPoint slides or transparencies are typi-

FIGURE 5.6.

Materials:	☒ Trainer's Tool Kit	☐ Transparencies	☒ Handout #1 <u>SRS Inventory</u>
		☒ PowerPoint file (& backup)	☐ Handout #2 _____
	☒ Leader Guide # <u>1</u>	☒ Name tents/tags # <u>12</u>	☐ Handout #3 _____
	☒ Workbooks # <u>12</u>	☒ blank ☐ pre-printed	

Purchased Materials: <u>SRS Inventory</u>   Date: <u>3/12</u>   Vendor: <u>Apex Inventories</u>

Reproduction: ☐ in-house ☒ outsourced   Vendor: <u>Kinkos</u>

☐ pick up ☒ to be delivered Date: <u>4/10</u>   to whose attention <u>me</u>   where <u>office/reception</u>

cal. Workbooks, handouts, or other support materials may be required for each attendee. In the example used for illustration here, a Supervisor Readiness assessment (filled in on the Program Planning Guide) will be used as a handout in class. Name tags or name tent cards should be available for each attendee. You may want to preprint attendees' names on their name tag or tent cards, or you may leave them blank and have the trainees complete them once they arrive at the training program (this is more an issue of style or time available than anything else).

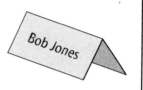

TIP A tent card is a heavy piece of paper or cardboard that, when folded in half, forms a tent that can stand on the desk in front of the trainee.

It is important to keep track of what materials you have purchased and when, where, and to whose attention they will be delivered. A good option when conducting training at an off-site location is to have the materials delivered directly to the facility. Shipping and delivery instructions vary from location to location—for instance, a hotel may request that deliveries be made to the receiving area, the front desk, or the sales office—so be sure to specify where your materials will be waiting for you when you arrive and to whose attention they were shipped.

Food and Beverage

Refreshments are critical to the success of any training program. If you don't think this is true, try holding a training session that starts at 9:00 A.M. and doesn't offer coffee. In the example in Figure 5.7, notice that the number of people used to calculate the amount of service needed is fourteen rather than the twelve attendees scheduled to attend training. When ordering food and beverages for training sessions, don't forget to include instructors or guest speakers in the total number of attendees.

FIGURE 5.7.

Food and Beverage: # 14

	☐ Mon	☒ Tues	☒ Wed	☐ Thur	☐ Fri	☐ Sat	☐ Sun
A.M. break	_____	10:30	10:30	_____	_____	_____	_____
P.M. break	_____	2:30	2:30	_____	_____	_____	_____
Lunch time	_____	12–1	12–1	_____	_____	_____	_____

☒ on-own, outside facility ☐ on-own, at facility ☐ catered ☐ facility provides
☐ working lunch ☐ separate room

Special needs? ☐ allergy   ☐ vegetarian   ☐ diet restrictions (list) _____

> **TIP** Susan Friedmann's book *Meeting and Event Planning for Dummies* (2003) has an entire (wonderful!) chapter dedicated to the nuances of planning food for meetings and training programs.

For a full-day program, you'll need to either provide lunch or allow a sufficient break to allow attendees to get lunch on their own. The "on their own" option is particularly attractive because it requires no extra work on your part and practically guarantees that everyone is happy with their lunch choice. However, it is important that you allow enough time for the trainees to get lunch, relax a bit, perhaps check their phone or e-mail messages, and get back to the training room in time for the afternoon session. If the training is conducted on-site, the lunch break does not have to be longer than your company normally allots for lunch; presumably your attendees arrange for their own lunch in this way each day. If the training is conducted at an off-site location, however, allow no less than sixty (and preferably ninety) minutes for lunch.

There are other options as well:

• *On their own at the facility.* Some hotel and conference centers offer a restaurant or a cafeteria that allows participants to stay on the property but relieves you from having to plan or pay for lunch. This option is also beneficial in getting participants back to the training room on time since they aren't going far.

• *Catered.* You may choose to have lunch brought in to the training session by an outside caterer. This option typically takes little time because the food is delivered and the choices are limited, allowing participants to get back to the training session quickly. It does require a bit of coordination on your part, however; you will have to choose a menu, and the caterer will need to know exactly what time you expect the food to arrive.

• *Provided by the facility.* Like using a caterer, you may choose to have the facility where you are holding the training provide lunch. This option also requires a minimal amount of break time and requires you to choose the menu. If you are having the facility supply lunch, you may consider having a working lunch where the food is brought in to the training room and the trainees eat at their desks, or lunch may be served in a room that adjoins the training room, which gives the participants more of a break.

Any option that requires you to choose a menu means that you also need to poll the trainees about any special dietary restrictions they may have. Allowing participants to get lunch on their own is the most expedient and the least expensive option for you as the organizer. Food is an important issue to individuals; when you distribute information about the training class, always be explicit when explaining the lunch arrangements.

Notes

The final section of the Training Program Planning Guide is used for any miscellaneous notes that pertain to your training session. In the example in Figure 5.8, the trainer has noted that it is important not to linger in the room after the training is complete on the second day, because the facility needs to get ready for another function.

FIGURE 5.8.

> **Notes:**
> Must be out of room by 5:15 on Wed — next group coming in

Summary

In addition to making sure you have addressed the essential details of planning a training program, using the Training Program Planning Guide allows you to delegate duties to others both inside and outside your organization. If reproduction will be done by the company mailroom, the materials and reproduction sections of the planning guide will assist those workers in creating the correct number of each type of material. An off-site facility will be helped immensely by the room arrangement and dates/times checklists. The entire checklist will assist you or an assistant in issuing invitations to participants that include essential information, such as the days, dates, and times of the training; where the training will be held; and whether lunch will be included. The Training Program Planning Guide also serves as a final checklist for the day of training to ensure that everything required to make the training a success is in place.

6

When and How to Choose Vendors and Outside Resources

THE DAY-TO-DAY REALITY for every accidental trainer is that there will be too much to get done in the hours that are available. You can be more effective by outsourcing some of your tasks and responsibilities by purchasing training products and services. By strategically choosing training solutions offered from vendors and other outside resources, you can serve your internal customers more quickly and free yourself for more critical tasks.

This chapter identifies vendor options and what you should consider, such as the cost or the fit with your organization, when choosing an external resource. It also provides a list of the types of vendors you'll want to research and have on call for those times when you need to outsource work.

> **TIP** Outsourcing uses external resources or products in order to meet needs and accomplish business goals.

Common Vendor Terms

Here are some common terms you will hear used by vendors or other training providers:

Contractor, consultant: Training and development experts used on a casual basis; not employees of your organization.

Customized: Training programs or products that are designed specifically for your organization's use.

Deliver, delivery: The actual presentation of a training topic.

Deliverables: An end product or interim pieces of a final product delivered by a vendor.

Off-the-shelf, generic: Training programs or products that are purchased and used as they are originally designed by the vendor.

Tailored: A training program or product that is adapted or modified to align with your organization's needs or culture.

Vendor: A supplier of training products or services.

The Make-versus-Buy Decision

The make-versus-buy decision is one that will frequently surface when your department's services are requested. The "make" decision requires creating a training program in-house from scratch. The "buy" decision relates to a variety of purchase options, which may include a complete program already designed or the custom design of materials on your behalf. For example, you may need to institute sexual harassment awareness training for your employees. Here are four possible "buy" options for the training:

1. Contract with a consultant or consulting company that has a prepackaged program. This company would provide the content and the trainer to come to your site to deliver the training.

2. Purchase a sexual harassment training program off-the-shelf. In this option, you purchase the content but are responsible for delivering the training. Delivery options include hiring a trainer or consultant to deliver the training package that you have purchased or delivering it using an in-house resource (yourself or another manager).

3. Purchase a self-study product such as a computer-based training program on the topic of sexual harassment in the workplace.

4. Find a public seminar on the topic, and send those individuals who need the training to the seminar.

TIP▷ Off-the-shelf training is generic training designed by a training vendor. You may purchase the rights to deliver the training at your site. Common off-the-shelf programs are found for sales training, customer service, and software programs.

I believe the mantra of the accidental trainer should be, "Don't reinvent the wheel." It is not always cheaper or faster to create a training solution in-house. You probably have neither the time nor the money to create a program that already exists or that would be suitable for your organization with a minimal amount of tailoring. Some of the considerations to assess when making the make-versus-buy decision are cost, time, content, and internal capabilities. Any one of these four issues can be a make-or-break decision about whether to outsource, and to whom. Taken together, they provide criteria to help you to organize your thoughts. I'll discuss each of them in detail, but keep in mind that the ultimate goal is the integrity of the training initiative.

Cost

The design of an effective training program requires a considerable investment in time, and time is money, as the saying goes. Even a simple one-hour course can require anywhere from ten to one hundred hours of design time when one factors in the time needed to research the topic, design the content and activities, create the materials, and possibly conduct an internal review with subject matter experts. If you factor together all of the hours required to design a training program in-house, you may find it is much more economical to purchase an intact training program or send your trainees out to a public offering on the topic. It is always more cost-effective to buy training when the topics you need are relatively generic, such as customer service, sales, or time management or for topics that are regulated such as sexual harassment awareness, Occupational Safety and Health Administration requirements, or hiring practices.

Time

Given the speed at which businesses today operate, the requests for training that you will receive often will not allow the time you need to design the training in-house. A one-hour training course that requires one hundred hours to design may take four weeks or more to design in-house when you must work it into your other training responsibilities. You may find that the buy decision is frequently the more effective way to get training out to the field in a timely way.

Another aspect of time to consider is the longevity of a program. If the topic is one that will be delivered on a frequent basis to employees, such as customer service skills or new supervisory skills, you may choose to develop the topic in-house because the development and delivery costs will be reduced over the life of the course, and the course will be customized to your organizational needs. A topic that will be offered to your employees only once, perhaps advanced negotiation skills, may be more economical to purchase.

Content

The appropriateness of the training content is the third decision factor. A generic topic or skill is most easily outsourced. Topics that are specific to your organization will require customized creation or perhaps tailoring of an off-the-shelf product. For example, a retail operation that wanted to train its managers in coaching skills found an off-the-shelf program that taught the concepts they were looking for but included a video of workers in an office setting. The training director was concerned that if the trainees did not see themselves in the video, it wouldn't have as much impact, so the vendor was asked to recreate the video and stage it in one of the retailer's stores. This increased the cost of the vendor-delivered course, but the additional expense was offset by the increase in quality that the customization provided.

Internal Capabilities

Sometimes a topic specific to your organization is beyond your capabilities or those of your organization and will require that you buy it. For example, a maker of printed circuit boards for the telecommunications industry wanted a generic course on the history of telecommunications and how its product supported the industry. Since there was no course available for purchase on this topic, it needed to be created in-house, but there was no one who worked for the organization who had the knowledge to design such a course. The organization ended up hiring an instructional design consultant to research and write a custom training program on the topic.

You may also find that a training vendor is more appropriate to deliver a topic to your organization. For example, even if you designed an advanced negotiation skills training course in-house for your sales department, would the salespeople respond well to your delivering it? And would you feel comfortable delivering it? In all likelihood, the best choice for delivering such a course would be an experienced salesperson or sales manager. You may be able to prevail on an individual with the appropriate skills from within your organization, or you may need to hire someone who possesses the skills and credibility you need.

Considerations for a Make-versus-Buy Decision

Carol McCoy, author of *Managing a Small HRD Department: You Can Do More Than You Think,* offers these decision factors when faced with a make-versus-buy decision:

Make	*Buy*
You have budget constraints.	Budget is available.
You have time to work with internal experts to develop the course and materials.	You have little time to develop the program or materials.

Make	**Buy**
The topic requires specific expertise found only inside your organization.	The expertise required is found only outside your organization.
Qualified credible resources are available.	Outside resources have more credibility as authorities on the subject.
Your organization can produce materials quickly and inexpensively.	You lack the capacity to produce the materials required to support the course.
Those in your organization tend to mistrust programs from the outside.	You need an objective perspective on the topic.
	A relevant, proven, tested, and credible program is available in the marketplace.

Source: Carol P. McCoy, President, McCoy Training and Development Resources and Find-Your-Roots.com, Falmouth, Maine. Reprinted with permission of Carol P. McCoy.

Types of Vendors

Given the time constraints that all businesspeople work within and the numerous responsibilities that you will tackle daily, it is important to find reliable vendors you can call on in order to provide quality service to your internal customers. I am using the term *vendor* in a broad sense to include any product or service for which you might contract. There are number of types of vendors that will be useful resources for you at one time or another—for example:

- Graphic designer
- Researcher
- Web developer
- PowerPoint expert

- Instructional designer
- Trainer or facilitator
- Printer
- Off-the-shelf content vendor
- Train-the-trainer content vendor
- Public seminar company

It's a good idea to meet potential vendors and understand the level of service that they can provide prior to needing them. This will reduce the stress level when you absolutely need a vendor and will increase the chances of selecting a quality provider through an advance, impartial analysis. You want to feel comfortable with the vendor or individual because you will be relying on him or her to make you shine in the eyes of the rest of the organization. Depending on the time frame or intensity of your project, you will often find yourself working long hours in close association with your vendors; you'll want to be completely at ease with your choices.

Graphic Designer

As the saying goes, a picture is worth a thousand words. A graphic designer can take basic ideas and make them into visuals that your audience can easily remember. When you are custom designing training, think about using the services of a graphic designer in order to make your training materials look as professional as possible, as well as to make your message easily understood. Consider the graphic in Figure 6.1, which depicts sales objections as an iceberg, with most customers' objectives hidden below the surface of the typical conversation. The image has a more powerful impact—one that trainees will undoubtedly keep in mind well after the training class has ended—than simply hearing the instructor say, "Most customers don't really voice their concerns and objections; we have to look beneath the surface."

FIGURE 6.1. EXAMPLE OF A WELL-DONE GRAPHIC.

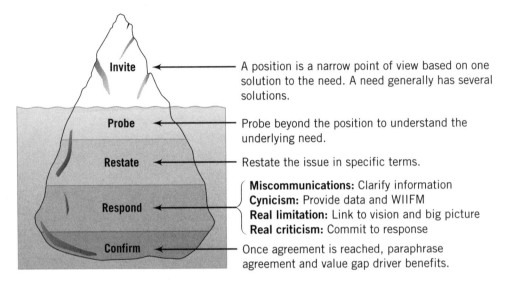

Researcher

A researcher is invaluable for searching out and collecting data to make your training accurate. A researcher can discover how many accidents per year happen in warehouses within the lumber industry or how much rework costs the semiconductor industry each year. I once was about to include information from a "well-known" study in a management training program I was designing, but first asked my researcher to find the origin of the study so that I could attribute it correctly. She quickly discovered the study was a well-worn management parable that was attributable to no one because so many "experts" were telling a different version of the "study."

Web Developer

Although Web programming can be relatively easy to learn, it is quite time-consuming and is better assigned to someone with that skill. Without even considering the complexities of e-learning, if you are posting handouts, PowerPoint slide sets, or other training materials on the Web, a Web developer will be invaluable to you—not only because your work will look professional but also because of the hours you'll save by not doing this relatively administrative task yourself.

PowerPoint Expert

A PowerPoint expert can help you create classroom visuals with impact. The rewards of using this expert are similar to those of using a Web developer: even if you are proficient at PowerPoint, creating your own slides can be time-consuming and adds little value to your role or to the organization. Paying someone who is an expert with the software is a wise investment both financially and mentally.

Instructional Designer

Instructional design is a labor-intensive process that requires long stretches of uninterrupted thinking time—something that is rarely afforded an accidental trainer. An instructional design expert will be able to take virtually any topic in any industry and create a learning process (course, video, or self-study program, for example) for it. Typically when you hire an instructional designer, it is a work-for-hire arrangement, which means that your company owns all rights to the material created. This type of arrangement allows you to design custom training materials that you have unlimited use of and to get them out into the field quickly.

Trainer or Facilitator

The delivery of training is a labor-intensive activity that may or may not require you personally. If the training topic is one that you are an expert at and for which you have credibility within the organization, you will probably be the best person to be the trainer. However, many topics can be effectively delivered by a skilled trainer or facilitator with no experience in the topic. In some instances, you may contract with a trainer that has his or her own program on a particular topic, in which case you are purchasing the whole package from one entity; in other cases, you may simply hire a trainer to deliver training that you have purchased from another vendor or created in-house.

A small utility company that was experiencing financial trouble created an in-house, classroom-based training program that asked every employee to minimize expenditures or suggest revenue-generating ideas the company might adopt. Tension in the company had been mounting for some time, and the workers were very vocal about the fact that they felt management had gotten them "into trouble" and it shouldn't be their own responsibility to get them out of it. Because the training department consisted of one individual, it would have required months for him to personally train everyone in the company, so he hired a group of facilitators (contractors) to conduct the training. Hiring multiple facilitators who had no connection to management or to the company benefited the training in two ways: multiple classes could be run simultaneously, and the facilitators were impartial in their delivery and did not take the side of management or try to defend its cost-cutting strategies but simply delivered the training.

Outsourcing the delivery of training courses is frequently a wise decision when you consider the number of hours that the delivery of training will take you out of your office and away from achieving the more global roles you are responsible for.

Printer

The copying, collating, and binding of your training materials is an administrative task that adds no value to your role in the organization. Finding a reliable and economical printer will relieve you of a tedious and never-ending task. Many printers also store your documents on their servers for future use and ship your documents to their final destination point. Chapter Four offers a list of useful resources in the "Technology Solutions" section.

Off-the-Shelf Training Product Vendor

Many training programs are generic enough that you can purchase them off-the-shelf for use within your organization. Rather than searching out topic-specific vendors each time you need a training program, find a broker who is conversant in many topics and represents many training vendors. Often one phone call to a training broker about your training need, such as clean room safety or the legal issues surrounding the Americans With Disabilities Act, is all that you will need to do; the broker will search out the best resources for you and suggest a short list of possible vendors. Professional associations that represent your trade are also a good source of prepackaged training materials that apply to your industry and the jobs within it.

Train-the-Trainer Content Vendor

One of the ways to maximize your training department's reach is to use other resources within your organization, such as managers and subject matter experts, as de facto trainers. Subject matter experts are best used when topics are technical or specific to a role. It is more expedient to use someone who is well versed in the topic than to learn the topic yourself so that you can then become the trainer. Managers are best used as trainers for topics of a managerial nature, such as leadership or ethics, and when your training would be assisted by the credibility or authority of such an individual. You may find that you would like these individuals to have basic trainer knowledge which is available through train-the-trainer (also known as T3) programs. These programs teach new trainers the importance of projecting their voice, using audiovisuals effectively, asking and answering questions from the audience, and other skills that are useful in conducting a training session.

Public Seminar Company

Many generic topics are offered through public seminar companies that produce full-day to multiday training programs in major cities throughout the United States. Topics are generic since the seminars are open to the public and there is no telling what types of industries will be represented in the audience. Topics range from time management to basic supervisory skills, project management, computer skills, and more. These types of vendors are useful when you have one or two individuals within your company who need specific skills training.

Choosing and Working with Vendors

In order to assess the services that potential vendors can provide, you will want to gather information about each vendor and compare their products and services. A well-thought-out selection process will ensure that you are comfortable with and confident in your selections.

Start by asking other trainers whom they rely on when they need the support of an external resource. You may want to create a consultant selection committee, much like the advisory committee discussed in Chapter Two, within your own organization, which will improve your choices and involve others in the selection process. Contacting and evaluating more than one vendor provides you with options and exposes you to a number of business methods and processes. Knowing about the range of services that each vendor provides, and what a working relationship with them would feel like, also gives you a backup strategy in an emergency should your vendor of choice fail you.

A Request for Information Worksheet (Worksheet 6.1) is designed to help you gather information from vendors that will provide services, rather than products, to your organization. It begins with a brief outline of your business situation and your expectations for the vendor and the product or service. The questions are broad enough to allow you to capture information from various types of service providers; however, not every question will apply to every type of vendor.

A request for information (RFI) is an important tool because it allows you to gather the same information from various vendors. If you were to simply contact a number of vendors and explain your needs, or if you were to go to vendors' Web sites to gather information about their products and services, you would have difficulty comparing one vendor to another because of the variety of ways in which they express themselves. The RFI allows you to gather the same information from multiple vendors and thereby have a more equitable comparison in order to make a decision. It first allows you to succinctly describe your situation and needs so that the potential vendor has a good understanding of what you hope to accomplish and how. The vendor question and response part can be used as a note-taking sheet while you are

---

WORKSHEET 6.1. SAMPLE REQUEST FOR INFORMATION WORKSHEET.

Your Situation

Brief explanation of the situation and what you wish the training solution to accomplish.

Anticipated start date: _____ and completion date: _____
or specific dates [for example, if you are hiring a trainer to deliver training]

Tasks and Deliverables [what are you expecting to receive, and when]

Assumptions/Limitations [for example, no personnel from your organization will be available to assist the vendor during the last week of each quarter]

Budget [you don't want to reveal this to the vendor too early in the process; however, you will need to have an understanding of what your budget is because it might allow you to reject vendors early in the process if their fees will be much more than your budget will allow. Nevertheless, budget should not be a defining factor too early in your discussions with the vendor because you may find that a higher cost results in a much greater return on investment for you. You want to give vendors a chance to fully explain their services and fee structure.]

What's the most important thing that you are expecting from this vendor? [saving you time, saving you money, teaching you new skills and knowledge, allowing you not to worry about the project?]

Is there anything the vendor should be aware of? [the program is sensitive or will have high visibility or has political implications?]

(continued)

WORKSHEET 6.1. SAMPLE REQUEST FOR INFORMATION WORKSHEET *(continued).*

Questions for Vendor	Vendor Response
Given our objectives, how do your products/ services match our needs?	
What past projects have you completed that are similar to our situation and needs?	
May I see samples of your previous work?	
I expect/would like to receive the following deliverables [list them]. Are you capable of providing each of these items?	
This project will roll out on [date], which means I will need all of the deliverables by [date]. Is this a deadline you can meet?	
Explain your work process. Will you work at our site or yours? What will you need from us in terms of space, personnel, and other items?	
Explain your review process. How many mile-stones do you expect? How will we monitor your progress? How do you prefer to receive feedback?	
Who will be working on this project?	
What roles will they play?	
Who will be my primary liaison?	
How do you charge: hourly, project fee, re-tainer, or something else? What do you expect this project, as I have explained it, will cost?	
How are expenses handled?	
If we experience overruns in cost or time, do you have a method for handling these situations?	
Who will the final work belong to? My company? Your company?	
How do you propose we evaluate the success of this program and the success of our working relationship?	
Do you have references available?	

on the phone with a vendor, or you can use it as a model to modify for your own specific needs and send it out to vendors by e-mail with a request that they complete it and send it back by a specific date.

Working with vendors, especially consultants who may be heading up a project for you, is not as easy as handing off work that needs to be done. It would be beneficial for an outsider to your organization to have background about your company—for example, how long it has been in business, the product or service you provide, your competition, your customers, employee demographics, and why this training project is a priority at this time. This type of information helps them to think more like a team member than an outsider. It's also a good idea to have a discussion about working style, communication preferences, check-in dates, deliverable expectations, and the like so that you don't find yourself frustrated, rather than relieved, by the use of an outside resource. I used to have a communication style of keeping quiet if things were going well; my belief was that I didn't want to bother my clients who were doing more important things. This made my clients *very* nervous. So now I check it quite regularly, even if all I have to say is that I have nothing to report.

Legal Considerations

In addition to determining what products or services to outsource to vendors, you should be aware of the rights and usage measures surrounding each product or service that you contract for. For example, purchasing an off-the-shelf training course or a video does not automatically give you the right to make copies; most packaged products of this type are copyrighted, and the copyright is retained by the vendor. Vendors can charge for off-the-shelf solutions in two ways:

- A per-use basis, which means that each time you conduct a training course, you are required to pay a fee or purchase participant materials for that course

- A site license that allows unlimited reproduction rights within your organization for a specified period of time

Should you have training materials custom designed for your organization, be sure to ask the vendor who will retain the rights to those materials; materials that you have created on a work-for-hire basis allow your organization to retain all rights to the materials. If you do not clearly specify this at the outset of your working relationship with the vendor, you may find that you are unable to use the materials you contracted for or you may find yourself in a battle for ownership. The box offers an example of an agreement you might construct between your organization and an outside resource. Check with your legal or HR department to see if there is a standard agreement already created that you can adapt for your needs.

Sample Agreement with a Vendor

AGREEMENT made this [current date], between [your company name], a company with its principal office located at [your company address] and [vendor company name], doing business at [vendor address].

It is understood that any and all copyright, intellectual property, and/or proprietary information gained or used during the course of this project remains with [your company name].

1. Project: [a brief description of the project, with the expected deliverables; suggestions are listed below]

   Deliverables:

   - Instructor Guide

   - Participant Workbook and handouts as necessary

   - Media including, but not limited to, PowerPoint sets, audio, video

   - One set of revisions upon [your company name] review of materials

   - One set of revision after first delivery of training program to client (pilot)

   Deliverables will be supplied via [do you want hard copies? CDs? e-mail attachments?]

2. Approximate Start Date:

---

3. Approximate Completion Date:

4. Total Project Cost:

5. Billing [options include payment on an hourly basis at an agreed-on rate, a fixed amount paid in installments, a retainer]

6. Services shall be rendered [will work be done at your facility? at the vendor's facility? both?]

7. Additional terms and conditions on next page.

Signatures

for [your company name]   for [vendor company name]

_____   _____

Individual with authority   Individual with authority

Resources

One of the most difficult tasks is to find resources and develop relationships before you need them. The Additional Resources section at the end of the book lists a number of resources in the areas of off-the-shelf training products, consultants or contractors, train-the-trainer programs, and other services that you may need. Begin slowly investigating each of these resources so that you are familiar and comfortable with what they offer before the time comes for you to call on them. Missing from this list of resources is your own industry's professional associations; be sure to investigate these associations as well to see what types of products or services they provide in the area of employee training and development because their offerings will be specifically tailored for your industry.

Summary

Creating and implementing a successful initiative is a big job, and sometimes it is beyond the physical capability of an accidental trainer to accomplish. When determining how best to get a training program off the ground, consider the investment in money and time, and then weigh the content and internal capabilities of your organization. The wise trainer will plan ahead and identify capable outside resources before they are needed. Another option you have to lighten your workload, besides contracting with vendors and other outside resources, is to take advantage of the many affordable resources available to you in your surrounding business community. The next chapter will help to assist you in locating these types of resources.

7

How to Provide Employee Training Without Doing It Yourself

IT IS MY GUESS THAT most of you turned to this chapter first! There's no denying that providing employee training is an essential component of business success. Without a continued investment in our employees' knowledge and skills, our competitors can quickly outpace us.

Even before you took on the training duties you now have, training was going on in your workplace; in fact, training is occurring in your organization right now. Most training that occurs in the workplace is informal. It happens on the job on a one-on-one basis. Studies that have tracked this phenomenon have determined that 80 percent or more of workplace learning occurs on the job, not in a formal training class.

This type of training occurs in two ways. One is what we trainers call "follow Joe around" training. A learner (usually a new employee) is paired with a more experienced worker who shows the new person the ropes. There is no formal agenda, and there is no guarantee that the information that is being transmitted is accurate or is officially sanctioned by your organization. The second is the more in-the-moment training that occurs when someone pops into a coworker's cubicle and asks, "Can you show me how to . . . ?" This type of training will never go away because every day, every one of us comes on something that we haven't had to deal with before, and we search out a solution at the moment we need it.

This chapter will help you to identify training opportunities that lie somewhere between the informal everyday occurrence and a formal full-blown training department, and that exist in your local area.

Low-Cost and Free Training Resources

Free and low-cost training programs are readily available from a number of resources in our own communities. In some cases, your trainees may need to travel to the training, and in other cases they will be able to take training, on demand, right from their own work area. Whether your employee needs are interpersonal or technical, you undoubtedly will find what you need by looking to the resources listed here.

Local Colleges

Many colleges are realizing that there's an untapped market in the individual who needs to gain a work-related skill, not earn a college degree. If you have just one or two employees who need training, check the noncredit or continuing education catalogue produced by your local college; these courses are always open to the public. If you have a group that is large enough (a dozen or so), most colleges will send instructors to your company to conduct training at your workplace. In both of these cases, the training programs are already available off-the-shelf, although you may be able to customize an offering if you are bringing it in-house.

In addition to prepackaged off-the-shelf offerings, community colleges are interested in working hand in hand with area businesses. For example, the community college in my town has created specialized training offerings in conjunction with local employers, including claims processing training for a Fortune 100 health care insurer and television production training for a well-known sports network. Neither of these offerings existed before the employers approached the community college for assistance.

Supplier and Client Companies

Suppliers are a great source of information as well as resources. Many suppliers already have training programs in place to train their own workforce. Simply ask if you can borrow their programs or perhaps pay a fee to use them with your employees. It's possible that your supplier's salespeople will conduct the training for you as well. For example, a retailer that was trying to create a more consultative salesforce in its footwear department requested assistance from its athletic footwear suppliers. A wealth of information was gathered from eight suppliers, including brochures, selling points, and videos. In another case, a salesperson for a liquor distributor who had a passion for wines offered a free one-hour training session to any of his restaurant clients that wanted to train their waitstaff. This training session was not an official offering of the liquor distributor but rather something that the salesperson was happy to do because of his interest in the topic and because he ultimately believed it resulted in more sales for him.

Public Seminar Companies

Public seminar companies provide all sorts of topics and courses for differing levels of employee need and proficiency. Technical skills range from how to use a software package to how to manage an IT project. Soft skills include customer service, performance appraisals, frontline supervisory skills, and more. These offerings are held in public venues, typically hotel ballrooms, and are quite generic because the seminar company has no control over the audience mix; various skill levels and industries will be represented. These types of training offerings are focused on knowledge more than skill, so that employees can bring back to the workplace and implement what they learned immediately. The instructors are superb and make the training experience a lot of fun. An added benefit of this type of gathering is the networking opportunities that are available to the employees that you send. See the Additional Resources section for a list of public seminar companies.

Video

There are two options for video: training videos that you purchase on a particular topic or videos that you create yourself at your own workplace. Purchased training videos exist for technical or operational skills such as how to safely operate a forklift or soft skills such as how to conduct a performance appraisal. Watching experts perform and model correct behaviors and techniques is one of the fastest ways to learn a new skill, especially an interpersonal skill. It's much easier to comprehend what it means not to use judgmental statements, for example, by listening in on a conversation that models the correct behavior than it is to try to imagine for yourself what that skill would sound like in practice.

> **TIP**
>
> *Soft skills* is a training industry term that is used to refer to interpersonal skills such as listening and feedback, stress management, and team building.

Creating a training video in-house does not have to be elaborate or expensive. You do not need expensive equipment or professional actors. All you need to do is videotape the best people doing the job the right way, explaining it step-by-step as the process is completed, and you have a training video. A manufacturing plant created all of its machine training in just this way. None of the machining processes was particularly complicated, but they were much easier to comprehend by watching the process rather than simply hearing an explanation of how the process should be completed. In addition, it was much too noisy on the manufacturing floor to conduct the training in that atmosphere. The training director used a handheld video camera to record the machine operator's processes and then recorded a one- or two-minute explanation of what the operator was doing to correspond with the video. In addition to showing an expert perform a skill correctly, another benefit of video-based training is that the trainee can refer to it as often as necessary.

The Web

The Internet is a wonderful resource. In addition to e-learning courses, which can be accessed on demand at sites such as CyberU (http://my.cyberu.com/home.asp) and e-Learning Center (http://www.e-learningcenter.com/index.htm), you can find free tutorials by using a search engine. Try various combinations of words, such as *tutorial, demo,* and *course* when searching—for example:

- Excel + demo

- Creating an Excel spreadsheet + tutorials

- Narrating a PowerPoint show + tutorial

- Unlawful workplace harassment + free online

- Safe lifting techniques + free online training

Microsoft also offers a wealth of software training, demonstrations, and tutorials for all of its Office products. Go to http://www.office.microsoft.com and look for "Training" in the left menu bar.

Associations

Professional associations are an often overlooked developmental resource. Most large professional organizations such as the American Society for Training and Development, the American Payroll Association, and the Association for Women in Communications have local chapters that meet monthly and offer speakers, seminars, and workshops on topics that are of interest specifically to their membership. Typically, dues-paying members of the chapter can attend these monthly events for free. Many professional associations also offer full-day workshops or conferences as fundraising activities at reasonable fees, such as the annual Southeast HR Conference, which is presented by the Atlanta, Georgia, chapter of the Society for Human Resource Management.

Government Agencies

Agencies such as the Small Business Administration and the Small Business Development Center exist to provide consulting to small businesses. Training is often one of the forms that the consulting takes. For more information, visit http://www.sba.gov/training/courses.html. Also, search out assistance that is offered through your own state's department of labor using the U.S. Department of Labor site at http://www.dol.gov/dol/location.htm. In addition, the federal government provides grants specifically targeted to workplace training.

Interns

High school and college interns are wonderful resources for training endeavors. Many institutions require their students to complete a workplace-related project. If your local college or university offers human resource or training degree programs, you are more than likely to find an individual, or perhaps even an entire group, who needs a placement site. Most often these resources are helpful in gathering and organizing data. An intern with a focus on training may even have the skills to design customized training.

I offered my own services for free to an organization when I was completing my doctorate in order to be able to structure my research in a way that supported my doctoral thesis. This arrangement provided tens of thousands of dollars of free consulting work to the company, which allowed me to use them for research purposes and to complete a project that I would not otherwise have been able to carry out.

Teleseminars

Teleseminars are similar to conference calls in that many individuals dial into a common number at the same time; however, teleseminars are usually designed for a large audience. The teleseminar, or teleclass, is conducted by an expert on a particular topic. This type of training typically lasts an hour or less. Similar to video-based training, you can find public offerings or create your own. The Accidental Trainer Web site lists free monthly teleseminars with training experts (http://www.TheAcccidentalTrainer.com). Recent topics have included:

• Tips and Techniques for On-the-Job Training: Fast, Low-Cost, Bottom-Line Results

- Preventing Death by Lecture! 12 Ways to Turn Passive Listeners into Active Learners

- How to Save Money on Outsourcing and Buying Products/Services for Your Training Department

The Institute of Management and Administration (IOMA.com) offers frequent teleseminars, called audio conferences, on operational topics; recent offerings for just one week included:

- Effective Performance Management

- Internal Controls for Credit Managers

- Best Practices in Lateral Hiring and Integration

You can find all sorts of teleseminar offerings that are free or have a modest fee. Start by looking at http://www.teleclass.com and http://www.teleclass international.com.

It's also quite easy to create your own teleseminars using internal experts. For example, a hospital that needed to update its entire staff on infectious disease control offered a thirty-minute teleseminar conducted by the education coordinator. The training consisted of an explanation of new policies, procedures, and assessment measures that were going into effect the following week. The education coordinator did not have time to create a training class and was concerned that issuing a memo would not be effective, especially if staff members had questions. The teleseminar training was offered numerous times over the course of two days, which allowed all employee and staff members to call in at their convenience. The seminar included twenty minutes of instruction and allowed ten minutes of questions from the audience. A similar offering could be conducted for a new product release, giving the sales force a quick tutorial on the features and benefits, or to assist employees in setting up a new computer at their desk rather than having the IT department visit each individual.

Teleseminars are wonderful learning tools because the learners can stay right at their desks. If you have a number of individuals who could benefit from the topic, they can all be trained at once by sitting in a conference room and using a speakerphone, all for the price of a single phone call. If your company does not have its own teleconferencing system, check into these two resources: http://www.freeconference.com or http://www.freeconference call.com.

Conferences

Professional conferences, which are produced by professional associations and typically encompass three or more days at destination locations, are a wonderful way to immerse oneself in learning. Conferences typically include general sessions that feature a well-known expert related to the theme or industry of the conference; concurrent sessions that are short (sixty to ninety minutes) and conducted by various practitioners and subject matter experts; half-day to full-day workshops on a particular topic, usually held immediately before or immediately following the conference itself; and special events, which can include plant tours or field trips to locations of interest to the conference attendees.

Conferences provide access to expert practitioners and networking opportunities with individuals who work in the same industry or perform the same type of work. Almost every conference offers audio recordings of the general and concurrent sessions so that you can bring home the speakers you enjoyed the most or to listen to the sessions that you were unable to attend because they happened concurrently. A search at http://www.allconferences.com under the topic of Manufacturing and limited to one specific month revealed a Food Packaging and Design summit, an international conference produced by the Association for Operations Management (APICS), a Steel and Ferroalloys conference, and seventeen others. To learn more about the field of workplace training, be sure to check out the annual American Society for Training and Development International Conference and Exposition (http://www.astd.org), the Society for Human Resource Management Annual Conference and Exposition (http://www.SHRM.org), and VNU/ *Training Magazine's* conferences that are held twice a year, once on the East Coast and once on the West Coast (http://www.vnulearning.com).

You don't necessarily have to search out all training opportunities for your employees. One relatively easy way to offer educational opportunities is through a tuition reimbursement program.

Tuition Reimbursement Programs

Tuition reimbursement is a wonderful first step in employee development for a number of reasons. First, it requires little effort on your part, or the part of the organization, other than to set up some guidelines that govern what types of courses are reimbursable. The majority of the work related to finding appropriate courses and registering for them is left up to the individual who wants to take the course. Tuition reimbursement typically applies only to college-level and for-credit courses; therefore, you probably want to ensure that the individual is working toward a degree that will benefit the organization. You don't necessarily want to reimburse a bookkeeper for your company for a course in astronomy, for example. A second reason that tuition reimbursement is beneficial to an organization is that attending college courses typically occurs during nonbusiness hours; therefore, your employee enhances his or her knowledge and skills without any impact on workplace productivity. A third reason to pursue tuition reimbursement is that the Internal Revenue Service allows employers to provide up to $5,200 per year in tax-free education assistance. Finally, tuition reimbursement is a wonderful policy because it will never hurt your company to have smarter individuals working for it.

TIP ► Tuition reimbursement is a refund or grant of tuition money for employees who are taking college courses. Usually enrollment in an accredited degree program is required.

A large manufacturing firm not only offers tuition reimbursement to its employees who are attending degree-granting institutions, it also allows those students to work only a half-day when they have class. This company is so committed to enhancing the educational level of its employees that it wants to ensure that everyone who is enrolled in a class has the time to get the assignments done.

Tuition reimbursement can apply to local colleges, community colleges, or universities. It may also apply to online universities and degree-granting institutions. In addition to local colleges in your immediate area, check out the U.S. Distance Learning Association (http://www.usdla.org) for resources and to provide direction to your employees. If you have enough students who are working toward a degree, you may be able to arrange with a local college to have the instructors come to you and to customize a delivery schedule outside of the standard sixteen-week semester.

A tuition reimbursement policy is an organizational commitment. If you choose to establish one, you will do so in conjunction with your HR department and the management or ownership of your company. Some of the things you'll need to take into consideration when constructing your policy are outlined in the box.

Tuition Reimbursement Considerations

- Who is eligible, and when?

    Full-time and part-time employees? If part time, how many hours at a minimum?

    Waiting period: ninety days after employment? A year?

    What if the employee resigns or is transferred midsemester?

- When is tuition reimbursed?

    At the start of the semester or after the course is completed and a grade received?

> Does it matter what the grade was? What if the employee flunks the course?
>
> • Are employees limited to certain institutions or degree programs?
>
>   Are online colleges acceptable?
>
>   Are employees limited to degrees in their professional field?
>
>   Must it be a two-year or four-year degree? Is a certificate acceptable?
>
>   What if the employee just wants to take a class that interests him or her?
>
> • What is reimbursable, and how much?
>
>   Just tuition? What about student fees, supplies, or software?
>
>   Is the employee reimbursed 100 percent of tuition or a percentage?
>
>   Is there an annual cap?
>
> • Will employees be given any discretionary time to complete course work?
>
> • When does an employee apply for reimbursement?
>
> • Is a term of service required on completion?
>
>   If your company just assisted an employee in getting a four-year degree, does it expect four years of continued employment in return?

In-House Library

One of the easiest ways to enable training and the transfer of knowledge within your organization is to begin an in-house library. I recently worked with a client in which I gathered data from several resources in order to design a training program. Although all of the information that I needed was in-house, I needed to go to the quality control department for some documents, the maintenance department for other documents, and the production office for additional information. Keeping all of the learning-related documents that the company owned in one place would have made my job easier and it would have been easier for learners within the organization as well.

Creating an in-house library does not have to be burdensome. You can start by gathering all of the individual subscriptions to which people within your organization subscribe; you may find that you are able to save the company a significant amount of money by canceling individual subscriptions and ordering periodicals and journals in the name of the company instead. Next, add all of the vendor-supplied resource materials that are undoubtedly scattered in different departments throughout your company. Finally, ask each manager within your company to add to a wish list. As funds become available, you can purchase books from this wish list to add to the library. You will probably want to organize the resources according to departments or topics—for example:

- Management
- Customer service
- Sales
- Marketing and advertising
- Career management
- Operations manuals and operational topics
- Industry-related topics
- Federal and state government references

You may also want to have an area in which you gather information regarding conferences and external training programs. An inventory kept on a clipboard and categorized in the same way as the resources (that is, by topic or department) should be periodically reviewed and organized to ensure that the library's inventory is maintained.

More Labor-Intensive Training Solutions

With a medium amount of effort—somewhere between starting a full-blown training department and the more expedient options outlined in this chapter—there are other ways to enable the transfer of knowledge within your organization. These options include:

- Formalized on-the-job training
- Coaching or mentoring
- Checklists and job aids

- Job rotation
- Using subject matter experts
- Creating discussion groups
- Pooling resources

Formalized On-the-Job Training

Formalized on-the-job training in essence organizes what is already occurring in your company. There is a natural transfer of information from one worker to another going on every day, without much forethought or planning. By creating a more structured job training guide, such as a training checklist for new employees, you can ensure a more formalized training process that covers the topics that you feel are crucial to a new employee's success. Figure 7.1 shows a sample of an on-the-job training checklist used by retail store managers when orienting a new employee.

FIGURE 7.1. NEW EMPLOYEE TRAINING CHECKLIST.

Description of Training	Trainer's Initials	Trainee's Initials	Date	Training Notes/ Follow-Up Needed
☐ Samples and Demos				
☐ Calendar				
☐ Health regulations				
☐ Maintenance				
☐ Demo equipment				
☐ Register				
☐ Register plan				
☐ Supplies				
☐ Maintenance				
☐ Sales floor				
☐ Customer-ready checklist				
☐ Stocking				
☐ Straightening				
☐ Cleaning				

Coaching or Mentoring

A number of studies have concluded that mentoring is second only to formal education in terms of determining an individual's success on the job. Many of us are aware that the baby boom generation is aging and gradually moving out of the workplace. Before our companies lose all of the knowledge and skills they have developed, it would be a wonderful idea to create a formalized mentoring process in which an older, more experienced worker is paired with a younger worker within your organization. Pairings might be assigned according to department and responsibility, or they might be more beneficial if they are interdepartmental. One large U.S. financial services firm created an internal mentoring program that requires all management associates to have at least one mentor at all times during their career with the firm. Higher-ranking managers volunteer to mentor at least one individual each year, and the program is organized so that a young manager will have a number of different mentors at different points in his or her career.

Checklist and Job Aids

Many times you will find that training is unnecessary so long as an employee has a checklist or job aid for guidance. Being able to change the toner in the photocopier is a perfect example of the usefulness of a job aid. No one has ever attended formal training on how to change toner, and yet all of us are able to do it, even when faced with a machine we have never seen before, because of the job aid that is printed inside the cover of every photocopier. Some jobs are done so infrequently that it isn't beneficial to conduct formalized training. For example, the payroll department of your organization must print W-2s and 1099s once a year. A checklist of steps to follow when the process needs to be conducted provides all the "training" that is needed and requires no organizational resources whatsoever.

Job Rotation

Job rotations enable employees of all levels within your organization to gain exposure to the different processes that are essential to your company's success. A well known U.S. manufacturing company has a formal four-year job rotation program that hires new managers right out of college and moves them through seven departments and roles during their four years of on-the-job training. Not only does job rotation give individuals a greater understanding of how your business operates, but it helps to cross-train the population for maximum efficiency and helps keep employees interested in employment with your organization because they're constantly learning.

Using Subject Matter Experts

Subject matter experts are individuals who work in your company and are the best at what they do. There may be no formal process of rank-ordering employees, but there certainly is an understanding of who is the best machine operator or customer service representative. Harnessing the knowledge and skills of these individuals and distributing it among the others who work in their division ensures that everyone learns from the best.

One way to do this is to develop a formalized process in which an exemplary staffer delivers a training session on one of his or her best practices. For example, a large insurance firm has its Rookie of the Year speak at each training class the following year to provide lessons learned and tips on how to be successful in the first year. You may also simply ask the person to document what he or she does in a step-by-step manner. An audit firm asked its best auditor to create a list of questions he asked during the interview phase of each audit because the answers he was able to get contributed to a more focused audit. You'll often find that subject matter experts are well regarded by their peers and serve as informal mentors or coaches long after training has concluded, which, in effect, allows the training to continue.

Creating Discussion Groups

Perhaps you would like to upgrade management skills within your organization. Rather than targeting a specific training topic, think about instituting a book discussion group in which a business book is read by all individuals in the group and a discussion is held after the reading assignment. One department manager of a midsized manufacturing firm instituted this type of training on her own initiative. The discussion group was started with a book that the manager chose, but then subsequent books were chosen by other members of the group. The manager reported observable changes in management behavior following the discussions that dealt with teamwork and communications.

Pooling Resources

Although at times it may not seem true, you are not the only individual faced with the challenges of keeping your employees' skills at peak efficiency. You may find other individuals or companies, both locally and within your industry, that would welcome the opportunity to pool resources in order to keep employees' skills at the highest level as well. One opportunity to find other companies with similar needs is within your local chamber of commerce. Although chambers of commerce are made up of many types of businesses, most businesses face the same challenges, such as enhancing efficiency, managerial skills, or computer literacy. If your company cannot afford to hire a consultant to deliver a training session on team-building skills, for example, perhaps pooling the resources of three companies that need the same type of training will enable you all to be successful.

The Manufacturing Alliance of Connecticut (http://www.mact.org), formed in 1992, pools the needs and resources of over a hundred small and midsized manufacturers and providers of services. The alliance can provide referrals to experts in the field of employee relations, staffing, and compensation and regularly offers training courses to which members of the alliance can send their employees.

Summary

Providing employee training does not have to be an overwhelming task. With a small amount of effort, it is possible to find resources virtually everywhere you look: on the Internet, over the telephone, and down the street. Providing your employees with an opportunity to strengthen their skills is not only a wise business decision on your part; it will be welcomed by your employees as well.

Creating Custom
Training Programs

I HAVE SAVED THIS chapter for the end of the book because creating your own training programs from the ground up is a complex process, and I encourage you to try the other options for providing training to your organization that have been discussed in previous chapters. However, if you are reading this chapter it is probably because your organization has a unique training need or topic that is best designed in-house. Creating training from scratch is time-consuming and intensive. There are degree programs, books, and entire companies dedicated to it. It is beyond the scope of this chapter to truly be able to teach you how to apply instructional design (as the field is officially referred to). My intent is to make the options and tasks easily understandable and doable for you, so that you are not overwhelmed by your training projects and you are successful in your endeavors.

The chapter is arranged in three sections; the first section provides a grounding in the theory behind how adults prefer to learn, the second gives an overview of the types of training you might create, and the last outlines the steps in the custom design of training courses with a focus on helping you to identify the correct questions to ask and the right data to gather. A foundation in the processes will help you to make better decisions when it comes to designing your own training.

How Adults in the Workplace Learn

When most of us think of training, we conjure up an image of a classroom with orderly rows of seating and an expert at the front of the room. While that may be an effective way for children to learn, it doesn't always match an adult's style, and it is not always an efficient way for learning to be disseminated in a workplace. Children don't have much lifetime experience to draw on, so it's difficult to ask them to reflect on a topic, and because their brains aren't fully developed, it's also difficult for them to make correlations between concepts or to extrapolate how something learned in the classroom might work in practice. Childhood education is arranged in a way that is more structured and relies less on the participants to move the class along. Adult learning is quite the opposite, especially workplace-oriented learning, where we want our learners to take the concepts from class and put them directly and immediately into practice on the job.

There is a field of study in this area known as adult learning theory, which has a number of tenets governing how adults best take-in and process information. In general, adults:

- Need to see the relevance of the training to their work

- Like to have some control over the learning experience

- Want to apply the training to their own experiences

- Want to be actively involved in the learning

- Learn best in cooperative situations

In practice this means that any training should be linked to their jobs so that the workers can see the relevance of it immediately; it should be interactive, allowing the trainees to discuss or work with the new information; and it should be a two-way communication between the leader of the class and the trainees rather than an expert who simply imparts wisdom. Although at least 80 percent of workplace training is conducted in the classroom, training does not have to be limited to a classroom environment led by an instructor. In fact, that type of training situation may be the most limiting in terms of getting information to the people who need it the most at the time when they most need it. The following section discusses various types of training that may be useful in getting knowledge into practice as quickly and efficiently as possible.

Types of Training

Training is whatever improves a person's knowledge or skills, as one of my experiences shows. While working on a PowerPoint presentation with a client, I noticed that she had printouts of each slide in full color. I remarked that it must have taken a long time for all of the slides to print, and she replied that indeed it did and she wished there were a better way. In the next minute, I showed her how to choose the "grayscale" option from the print options window in the software program. Did I train her? I think so. Does she have more knowledge? Yes! Did she learn a new skill? Yes, again! Will it change the way she works with this software application forever? You bet! Training can be in the moment, on the fly, and just in time, so don't limit your options by thinking "classroom" when your workers might be better served by other methods:

- On-the-job training
- Self-directed training
- E-learning
- Job aids and worksheets
- Use of subject matter experts

As I explain each of these approaches, think about how you might use them to your advantage in your organization.

On-the-Job Training

On-the-job training typically pairs a more experienced worker with a new or less experienced worker. This type of training is effective when there are only a few new learners. For instance, most fast food restaurants conduct on-the-job training because although there is always a steady stream of new employees, the company cannot afford to wait until there are enough of them to form a class; it is important to get the new person on the floor and being a productive member of the crew as quickly as possible. This approach is typically conducted in a "follow Joe around" manner, which can result in inconsistent training at best and perhaps erroneous training at its worst.

If on-the-job training is the best approach for you, consider using checklists for both the "instructor" and the trainee so that there is an organized flow of information and you are able to ensure that all necessary topics are covered. Figure 8.1 shows an example of a training checklist for a new employee in a retail establishment; in this instance, the store manager would train the employee on a one-to-one basis.

Self-Directed Learning

Self-directed learning, also known as self-paced or independent learning, is learning that is accomplished independent of others and at the learner's own

FIGURE 8.1. NEW EMPLOYEE TRAINING CHECKLIST.

Description of Training	Trainer's Initials	Trainee's Initials	Date	Training Notes/ Follow-Up Needed
☐ Samples and Demos				
☐ Calendar				
☐ Health regulations				
☐ Maintenance				
☐ Demo equipment				
☐ Register				
☐ Register plan				
☐ Supplies				
☐ Maintenance				
☐ Sales floor				
☐ Customer-ready checklist				
☐ Stocking				
☐ Straightening				
☐ Cleaning				

pace. Although most of us do not think of it in this context, most of our learning beyond our formal education is done in a self-directed way. Many home improvement projects are really self-directed learning projects. A learner who decides that now is the time to take on new knowledge or skills doesn't want to wait for a class to form on the topic. In fact, isn't one of the reasons you bought this book that you needed a way to learn about the field of training and your role within it? Figure 8.2 shows an example of a self-directed learning manual. The topic was a proprietary software product, and the audience was an outsourced firm in India that was used to process data for the company that designed the software.

FIGURE 8.2. EXAMPLE OF A SELF-DIRECTED LEARNING MANUAL.

In this section you will learn to:
- ☐ Download files through FTP transfer
- ☐ Unzip (extract) files using WinZip

Steps		Notes

Begin by creating a data folder on your hard drive.
 	
Create all the folders and subfolders pictured here.
	Folders
	☐ Desktop
	  ☐ My Documents
	  🖥 My Computer
	    💾 Local Disk (C:)
	    ☐ Data
	    ☐ Training
	      ☐ Forms
	      ☐ Parsing
	        ☐ Parsing Practice 1
	          ☐ Problems
	          ☐ Samples
	        ☐ Parsing Practice 2
	          ☐ Problems
	          ☐ Samples
	      ☐ Splitting
	        ☐ Split Practice 1
	        ☐ Split Practice 2
		All clients are identified with a 4 digit-3 letter code, such as: 4900-ICA.
		
		In the future, when working with clients, you will create a folder with the client name, rather than "Training." This is where you will download all your data while working with that client.

From the Windows desktop, double click on FTP Pro	**WS_FTP Pro**	This will launch the FTP Pro. Connect to *Remote Host* window (see illustration next page)

Computer-Based Training

Computer-based training (CBT) and e-learning are broad terms that refer to any knowledge delivered electronically. This may include a course accessed and taken over the Internet, a course that is accessed using a CD or DVD at the learner's desk, or even live instruction delivered in what is known as a synchronous environment. You've undoubtedly experienced e-learning numerous times when you've used the Help function of any software program. E-learning may be both self-directed or part of a more structured course. The creation of computer-based training is the most time-consuming and expensive option for training design. It may require special software in order to construct, and it most certainly requires a large investment in time. A conservative estimate for a relatively easy e-learning design (for example a self-directed PowerPoint show with embedded audio) would be forty hours of design time to one hour of instructional time. There are a number of software products available to assist in the design of e-learning listed in the Additional Resources section. You may wish to visit The Accidental Trainer Web site (http://www.TheAccidentalTrainer.com) to view samples of e-learning as well.

Job Aids and Worksheets

I like to think of job aids as cheat sheets. These are quick reference materials that help learners accomplish or remember how to do a particular task. When you buy a new piece of computer equipment, it typically comes with an extensive manual and a Quick Start guide (a.k.a. job aid) as well. Voice mail prompts are another example of a job aid. Whenever we are confronted with a new voice mail system, we rely on the prompts to help us retrieve, delete, or repeat messages. Eventually we memorize the steps and no longer need the job aid.

Worksheets are similar to job aids except they are more extensive and usually are designed to be a fill-in-the-blank form rather than a checklist or instructional piece. The Internal Revenue Service form you complete each year in order to file your income taxes (in the United States) is an example of a worksheet. Although the form comes with a separate instruction package, instructions may also be embedded in the worksheet you design. Figure 8.3 is useful in planning a corrective action conversation with an employee. This book is full of worksheets that will help you to do your job in a well-thought-out and consistent way.

FIGURE 8.3. CORRECTIVE ACTION WORKSHEET.

Individual: _____

Behavior to address: _____

Is there a standard for performance?   Yes ☐   No ☐   What is it? _____

Does the worker know the standard?   Yes ☐   No ☐

What specific, observable facts or data do you have to back up the substandard performance?

_____

_____

_____

_____

What impact do his or her actions have on his or her own performance, the team, the company, or its goals?

_____

_____

_____

_____

What are the consequences (if any) if the behavior does not change?

_____

_____

What are your suggestions for a solution?

_____

_____

How will you start the conversation? How will you let the worker know the purpose of the conversation?

_____

_____

_____

One of the most crucial decisions you will make when it comes to designing your own training is determining the best method for delivering the training. Classroom training is just one option among many. Some factors that will help you make a choice are the complexity of the job, the frequency of tasks, the number of people who require training, how quickly training is needed, and the resources you have available.

The Process of Training Design

Instructional design (ID) is the process of designing training for the purpose of teaching new knowledge or skills. Typically ID is practiced in the workplace; a similar version is carried out in academia, where it is known as curriculum design. Instructional design begins with an expected outcome in mind, for instance, the ability to keyboard, and then creates learning that enables the trainee to achieve the outcome. All sorts of considerations need to be addressed when planning the design of the instruction:

- The existing ability level of the trainees

- How far they need to come to achieve success

- Whether they are capable of achieving success

- What will happen if they cannot do the new task

- The ramifications of not conducting the training

To a novice, instructional design looks rather easy. In fact, it is quite a complex process to ensure that the training process results in the outcome you are expecting.

There are a few instructional design methodologies in use today. The most frequently used and referenced method is known as ADDIE. ADDIE stands for:

A—(Needs) Analysis or Assessment

D—Design

D—Development

I—Implementation

E—Evaluation

ADDIE outlines the five foundations of instructional design and will be the framework around which the remainder of this chapter is constructed. Depending on the nature of the training, you may find that you do not use every step; however, it's important to understand each step and how each informs the following step in order to be able to make a knowledgeable decision about its appropriateness in your own organizational environment.

All training that you design should ultimately be focused on worker accomplishment and performance. The method of creating and delivering that training should be secondary to the outcome: increased knowledge and skill on the part of the learner. So first, you need to know where learners are lacking. This is accomplished with a needs analysis.

Needs Analysis

I believe that a needs analysis is the most crucial step in the custom training design process. The reason I give it such weight is that a properly conducted needs analysis can save you from the other steps if it turns out that the issue at hand is not truly a training issue. For example, in an earlier chapter I related a story about an inside sales team that had to undergo customer service training when in fact the real issue was a crucial piece of equipment that was missing from their department. Had they possessed this piece of equipment, they would not have had the volume of customer complaints that compelled the thinking that customer service training was needed. A simple needs analysis, which could have been done in less than a day by talking with some of the workers and watching them as they worked, would have quickly identified the true problem with this department.

The next time a manager within your organization approaches you with the idea that his or her workers need a particular training class, combat the instinct to immediately agree. Instead, put on your consultant's hat and begin to ask questions of the manager making the request, the workers who perform the tasks, and others within the organization who may have had a chance to observe or work with the department and may have insight about what the issue truly is.

I once was contacted by a retail organization that thought its buyers did not know how to use the software necessary in their jobs. Their "evidence" was that the end-of-month reports produced by this group were always wrong. After speaking with the trainer (who did an excellent job of explaining how to use the software), two representatives of the "problem group," and a senior-level manager who was a recipient of the erroneous reports, I was able to determine that the buyers lacked basic math skills. They knew how to use the software, but since they were populating the software with incorrect data, the reports simply reflected a case of "garbage in, garbage out."

Another useful aspect of the needs analysis is to help distinguish between needs and wants. Often managers say they want time management, stress management, or communications skills (perhaps because these are popular topics) but the organization doesn't truly need these. Although there is nothing wrong with providing employees with knowledge and skill that fall under the category of "wants," given the limited amount of time and resources available to you, you have to set priorities. You don't want to divert resources away from needs in order to satisfy wants.

The needs analysis will guide you in your decision whether to apply a training solution and what type of training to apply. More often than not, you will be assessing a group's needs based on a request from their manager. You'll want to probe the manager for information about why he believes he has a training problem in order to ensure you can assist. The questions listed below are a good starting point for your conversation with the manager.

Questions to Ask the Manager

- What leads you to believe that this training request is indeed a problem for your employees?

- How does the employee receive information or direction in order to complete his or her job?

     How often does the information change?

- What type of feedback do you provide for workers who perform poorly?

- Is there a standard operating procedure for the job?

  Have all employees been trained on it or have access to it?

- Do you consider this a simple or complex task, or something in between?

  Tell me more about the complexities of the task. What are the variables?

- Is your department adequately staffed?

- Do workers have all of the tools necessary to perform their work?

- What process or procedure precedes your workers' job? That is, where does their work flow from?

- Where does their work flow to?

- Is the workload or deadline reasonable?

- What are the consequences for poor performance?

You may also wish to ask the employees how they feel about the situation. I find it useful to talk with at least three individuals; I usually ask the manager to let me speak with his "worst," "best," and an "average" worker.

Questions to Ask Workers

- Do you understand what the expected output of your position is?

  What is it?

- Do you believe you have been adequately trained to perform your job? If no, what do you need?

- Do you have all of the information you need to do your job correctly?

  How accurate is that information?

  Do you receive the information with enough time to perform your job correctly?

  What information are you missing?

- Do you have all of the tools you need to do your job correctly? If no, what do you need?

Often you'll want to observe employees as they go about their work. You may be able to identify a process issue that has nothing to do with knowledge or skill, as in the case of having the fax machine down the hall.

Observations. Observe two or three individuals performing the job at different times of the day (work conditions sometimes change according to the time of day). Note differences in their speed, efficiency, output, and ease with which they conduct their work. Be sure to ask each of the workers the questions outlined above. You may find that the "more skilled" worker is getting information from someplace other than the official source. Maybe this worker has a connection in another area that puts him or her at an advantage (and that would be beneficial if everyone knew). Alternatively, you may find that all of the "unskilled" workers have been trained on the job by the same individual.

Not all training needs are due to a lack of employee skill or a problem in the workplace. You may want to take the pulse of the organization simply to see what people are thinking and what opportunities there may be for training. This approach to training can be accomplished using surveys, advisory councils, and data analysis.

Surveys and Polls. You may want to poll the employee population about what skills they would like training for in the coming year. Use a survey or questionnaire that offers a number of suggestions and asks the respondents either to check all of the topics they would be interested in or to rank-order three topics they would be most interested in. The same questions can be asked of management for themselves (What would you like to learn?) and for their employees (What do your workers need?).

Focus Groups and Advisory Councils. A focus group or advisory council is made up of individuals who represent the rest of the organization in decisions that deal with training. You probably have similar groups in your organization that meet regarding workplace safety or succession planning. Advisory councils, which consist of individuals from various departments and ranks within the organization, meet on a regular basis to discuss training needs that they have observed or that they have been approached about. (The organization of an advisory council was discussed in detail in Chapter Two.) Focus groups are a one-time gathering with a specific agenda or topic to discuss. Either group can assist you in determining training needs and prioritizing them. This approach is very useful because it relieves you from having to make all of the decisions. A group of peers who have a big-picture view of the organization can guide decisions about the need for training.

Data Analysis. Information that your company already gathers may provide useful insights into training needs as well. For example, an assessment of the payroll records of a service firm that suffered 100 percent turnover on a yearly basis identified that most employees left before completing thirty days of employment. The company was then able to identify common factors among those employees who left such as age (more teenaged workers left than older workers), prior work experience (those who had never worked before were more likely to leave than those who had held a job in the past), and the distance that employees lived from the workplace (employees who lived outside a ten-mile radius tended to quit more often than those who lived nearby). The company was able to modify its hiring strategies based on this data analysis, as well as institute a better orientation for new employees so that they felt more connected to the organization. In all likelihood, the orientation alone would not have solved the problem. It was important to identify that there was more to the company's turnover problem than whether the new employee felt welcomed and connected.

The purpose of a needs analysis should focus not only on what type of training needs to be created but also should answer the question, "How do I know that training is the right solution?" The Institute of Management and Administration cites training needs assessment as one of the most successful cost-control strategies a training department can employ. Once you have determined you have a training need, you'll want to design an approach to resolve it.

Design

One of the first decisions to be made in this step is determining what format should be used to deliver the training to the trainees. Several options were discussed at the beginning of this chapter. You will not achieve positive results if the training design and methodology are poor. For instance, when operational topics such as how to operate a machine or how to complete a form are the subject of the training, participants should work with the materials they would be expected to use on the job (the machinery, the form). Showing a picture of the machine and pointing out its component parts won't be sufficient. Interpersonal skills, such as giving performance reviews or managing conflict, should use role plays and realistic practice situations. Skills that require group interaction such as self-directed teams or project management should be designed so that a group takes the training. These are not the types of topics that lend themselves well to a self-directed training program.

A large cable network made an organization-wide switch to a new e-mail platform that required everyone in the company to have training on the topic. The IT department decided that the best training option was to gather people together in a conference room—with no computers—and demonstrate how the new e-mail program worked by demonstrating its use using a laptop and projecting the image on the wall. One IT staffer was assigned to roam the headquarters making his presentation, two hours at a time, floor by floor, until the entire twenty-five-hundred-person company had been "trained."

The IT department was dismayed at the low turnout at the training classes and frustrated by the fact that the employees didn't "see the importance" of attending the training. In reality, after the first presentation or two, word got out that no one actually learned how to do anything in the training. It wasn't training; it was a presentation.

In this case, two other options would have been much more viable. The first would be to conduct group training sessions in a training room with computers for each individual in attendance. The other would be to create a self-studying tutorial that demonstrated exactly what the trainer in the conference room demonstrated and make it downloadable from the company intranet or distributed on CD. This option would have allowed each employee to take the tutorial at his or her own pace, immediately practice on his or her own computer, and review the information as many times as necessary.

By spending the time required to think through the design of your training, the most appropriate delivery method should become clear. Next, you'll want to consider what gets included in the training. This will require a review of resource materials and speaking with subject matter experts (when available). As you determine what will be included in the training, you'll begin to:

- Clearly define the outcomes or objectives of the training
- Sequence the content
- Identify areas of knowledge versus areas of skill
- Identify necessary practice
- Identify how you might evaluate trainees' success

Each of these considerations is explained below.

Clearly Define the Outcomes or Objectives of the Training. There's an old saying, "If you don't know where you're going, how will you know when you get there?" Essentially this is the gist of clearly defining the outcomes of your training. The most crucial thing you can do during the design phase is to write objectives that clearly state what trainees will leave the training knowing or doing that they didn't know or couldn't do before. Objectives always begin with a verb. Here are a few examples:

"Identify the major bones in the hand."

"List the supplies needed in order to assemble a go-cart."

"Recite the lyrics to the song 'Yesterday,' by the Beatles."

"Change the oil in a car."

Some objectives might need subobjectives, as in the case of "change the oil in a car." Subobjectives might be:

"Identify the tools needed."

"Identify the correct weight oil required."

"Correctly dispose of the waste oil."

A well-stated objective will allow an observer to identify whether the trainee has indeed learned from the training. For example, if I am given a lyric sheet, I will be able to determine whether someone has correctly recited the lyrics to the song "Yesterday."

Sequence the Content. Next, consider in what order the content should be taught. For example, in a manufacturing environment, it would be important to learn safety procedures before learning how to operate the machinery. When changing a car's oil, it's not as important to learn the tools before the process or vice versa. The box offers a number of options for sequencing content.

Ways to Sequence Training	*Example*
Known to unknown	Financial software training begins by making a comparison to a checkbook and allows participants to become comfortable by writing checks and using the register to balance their checking account. It then progresses to the other functions of the software.
Easy to difficult	Piano lessons start by teaching individual notes and playing scales, and progress to reading music.
Frequent to less frequent	Cash register training begins with handling a cash payment, then a credit card payment, and finally a payment by check.
Problem to solution	Computer training begins by diagnosing the problem and then applying the correct solution.
Step-by-step	Cardiopulmonary resuscitation (CPR) training follows a strict protocol of steps.

Identify Areas of Knowledge versus Areas of Skill. Every training class will contain some new knowledge and some new skill. As in the example of changing the car's oil, identifying the tools that are needed and the correct weight of the oil are both knowledge objectives. These two concepts form the foundation of learning to change a car's oil; this knowledge will serve one well no matter what make of car. However, the skill of actually changing the oil will be dependent on the type of car one is working on. Separating the knowledge from the skill allows the trainer to determine the best way to deliver the new information. You may choose a classroom setting to teach about the tools and the weights of oil. There really is no need to have the machinery (in this case, a car) available in order for trainees to master the knowledge. Alternatively, these two topics don't necessarily require a classroom or group learning at all. You could also put this information in a booklet and require the trainees to read it in advance of coming to the training.

Identifying areas of knowledge versus areas of skill is important for two reasons:

1. You are better able to define the best delivery method for each topic or objective.
2. You are able to identify the correct sequence for teaching the topic.

Although both the knowledge and the skill portions of changing a car's oil are important, there is no clear requirement that one be taught before the other. You may choose to teach your trainees how to change the oil first because you know that they are a hands-on group and would be more motivated to learn by being able to play with the machinery first. You may then follow the skills portion by saying, "Before you can change the oil in a car, it is imperative that you understand how to choose the correct tools and correct weight of oil. Therefore, we will now learn . . ." Your trainees may be more motivated to absorb the knowledge portion of the training now that you've impressed on them that they cannot do the skill portion correctly without having the knowledge as well.

Identify Necessary Practice Areas. People learn best by doing; virtually every training topic will require some element of practice. Depending on the complexity of the topic, the practice may be brief, such as allowing ten minutes for new airline reservationists to practice making a reservation, or it may be extensive, such as a half-day lab that allows trainees to practice repairing a photocopier.

As you conduct your needs analysis, you will begin to get a sense of what objectives will require trainee practice and how much time should be devoted to the practice. Practice is essential if you expect trainees to return to the job and be able to implement what they have just learned. Remember the story of the e-mail training that did not allow the trainees to work with the software. This training design set up the trainees for failure.

Use this basic model when designing training that incorporates all of the above elements:

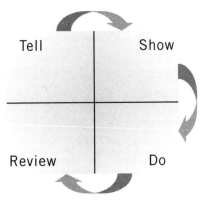

TELL and SHOW incorporate knowledge objectives, DO incorporates skill objectives and practice, and REVIEW ensures that the trainees understand both the knowledge and the skill.

Plan to Evaluate Trainees' Success. The final part of the design phase requires you to give some thought to how you will know if your trainees have been successfully trained. Will you give them a test? Watch them perform a new job or task? The evaluation should be closely aligned with the training. For example, a course on the history of telecommunications would lend itself to a written test, and a course on CPR would lend itself to a demonstration of the skill. In the case of changing a car's oil, a performance test is all that would be needed. While it would be possible to give a test in which the trainee had to identify the correct tools to be used, that objective is just as easily evaluated by observing that the trainee chooses the correct tools in the process of demonstrating that he or she can change the oil. It is helpful to identify how you will evaluate the training during the design phase because as you begin to develop the training (the next phase), you will find many opportunities to create the evaluation at the same time.

Development

Now that you have conceptualized the design of your training, the development phase answers the question, "What does it look like?" and requires you to begin to develop the materials. Elements that are created in this phase include:

- Course materials (workbooks, handouts, videos, and so forth)
- Leaders' guides
- Learning activities
- Support materials such as visuals and learning aids
- Tests or other assessments

Design, development, and implementation blend together in many respects. For instance, during the design phase of an orientation program for new employees at a retail store, the content was gathered, the sequence was determined, and it became apparent that the store managers had no time to train a new employee, so the training would have to be largely self-study. The development phase then addressed the questions, "What does the self-study program look like? How will learners access and work with the new information?" The deciding factor in what form the materials would take encompassed how the training would best be implemented. The training consisted of knowledge and skill; the knowledge could be learned independently, but the skills portion needed an expert's guidance and practice time for the learner. The final form of the training program was a combination of PowerPoint slides with voice-over audio that the new employee would view independently for ten minutes. Each ten-minute segment consisted of one concept and ended with a list of action items for the new employee to go out onto the retail floor and discover or practice. This implementation process was decided on to allow the training to be conducted in the store with the store manager nearby in order to assist the new employee, monitor his or her progress, and answer any questions.

Another consideration during the development phase is how the training materials will be maintained and distributed. For a subject that requires frequent updating, perhaps something that deals with federal regulations, distributing print materials would be cumbersome and costly. In addition, there would be no way to ensure that the old materials had been destroyed. In this situation, the best development approach would be to store the training materials on the company's server so that they could be accessed by any employee at any time and so that the training department could be confident that trainees were always receiving the most up-to-date information.

Remember that you don't necessarily have to develop all of your materials. Look to suppliers, vendors, or similar companies that might already have components you can incorporate into the custom design of your training. You may recall from earlier chapters that Shoe U used information and videos gathered from athletic footwear manufacturers and a department of transportation training project collected training materials from various states' transportation departments to use as a model.

Implementation

The implementation phase involves rolling the training out to the employees. More administrative-type details to consider during the implementation phase are scheduling the training rooms, scheduling employees to attend the training (for instance, in a call center environment, not everyone can leave the floor at the same time), producing and shipping the training materials, and tracking attendance. These details are required whether the training is developed in-house or is a purchased program.

Pilot tests frequently kick off the implementation phase of a training rollout. A pilot test is used with a sample of employees in order to see if the design does indeed work as expected and how employees receive the training. A pilot is typically conducted two or three weeks in advance of the full-scale rollout of the training. This allows time to revise and refine any issues identified as problematic by the pilot group. For example, a sales manager training program incorporated a video that showed a sales manager having an inappropriate coaching conversation with a salesperson and then showed the correct way to have the conversation. Feedback from the pilot group indicated that they saw no value in watching the video of the correct behavior; they felt it was more valuable to watch the inappropriate conversation and have a discussion regarding what elements the manager should correct if he were to have the conversation again. The trainees were essentially saying they didn't want to be fed the right answer; they wanted to figure it out on their own. This feedback required a change in the training design as well, so an activity, discussion, and debriefing needed to be created in order to allow the sales managers the experience they wanted.

The actual implementation of a program will probably identify gaps in planning and uncover logistical tasks you didn't consider. Make certain you have built in time to accommodate these small bumps and document what you did (and how!) for the next time. Training design is an iterative process, and the implementation of a program should be considered an opportunity to improve the process. The next step, evaluation, is your opportunity to improve the design.

Evaluation

Once you have implemented a training program, you'll want to know whether it was effective. The final step of the ADDIE approach to design is evaluation. The expectation is that the training was implemented in order to enhance or change employee work performance, so the evaluation phase will help you determine if that happened. Evaluations can take many forms, including:

- Objective tests
- Tests of skill
- Performance results
- Business results
- Return on investment

The type of evaluation chosen will often correspond with the training design. For example, in order to determine if a trainee can actually change a car's oil, a test of skill would be the best evaluation choice (can he do it?).

Objective Tests. Objective tests are the tests that most of us are used to from our school-
ing: fill in the blank, multiple choice, and true-false. Objective tests may also
ask the learner to review information (such as a case study) and draw a conclusion, make a decision, or construct a list of recommendations. Objective
tests are used to evaluate knowledge—and, more accurately, the ability to
recall information—that the learner has gained during the training session.

Tests of Skill. Tests of skill are more appropriate when the learner has learned a process
or procedure. A test of skill might ask the learner to assemble a computer cen-
tral processing unit by using a schematic or to demonstrate her ability to ask
open-ended questions appropriately in a role play. A skills test ensures that
the learner can apply the knowledge and complete the process just learned.

A manufacturer of office machinery put its field service reps through a four-and-
a-half-day training program that taught them how to install and customize,
according to a client's request, a software package that was an add-on to the
client's existing machinery. Although the training program included many hours
of practice for the trainees, the final evaluation was a paper and pencil test. Over
70 percent of the trainees failed the final evaluation. Since the course had spent
the majority of the time teaching them to install and manipulate the software,
the final exam should have given them an installation and customization request
and asked them to perform the installation as they would be expected to do at
the client site.

Performance Results. A performance evaluation is similar to a skills evaluation, but it is
not done until the trainee has returned to the job and then evaluates whether
that person has successfully transferred the knowledge and skills learned during the training to his or her work responsibilities. For example, an appropriate evaluation of a time management training course would be a
performance test. While it would be possible to apply an objective (knowl-

edge) test to determine if the trainee understands time management concepts and it would be possible to apply a skills test to observe whether the trainee can plan and prioritize tasks, the true test of whether the trainee has internalized the new knowledge and skills is that he or she uses time management techniques back on the job. Performance result evaluations are more cumbersome to conduct because they require checking back with trainees a few weeks after they've returned to the job or asking for the trainee's manager to report on any apparent performance improvements, but they are the best indicator of whether the training is taking hold in the workplace.

Business Results. Business result evaluations are more data driven and look for a change in business output or work performance that occurred as a result of the training. A retail organization that trained its regional human resource managers to recruit and interview store managers resulted in pushing that responsibility down from the corporate office to the regional offices. This successful distribution of responsibilities was exactly the business result the training had hoped to achieve.

Rather than evaluate a specific individual, as the previous evaluation methods do, business result evaluations take a step back and assess the impact the training has on the organization. Business result evaluations, like performance evaluations, also require a period of implementation before a valid assessment and evaluation can be conducted.

Return on Investment. A return on investment evaluation determines whether the training was worth the investment. To continue with the human resource example, one of the results of pushing recruitment and interviewing from the corporate level to the regional level was that an in-house corporate recruiter position was eliminated. This one business result alone resulted in savings to the corporation of forty-nine thousand dollars. The total cost to design and deliver the training to the human resource regional managers was $17,000.00. Clearly the training project had a positive return on investment.

Worksheet 8.1 will help you organize your thought process while you are creating a custom-designed training program.

WORKSHEET 8.1. TRAINING DESIGN WORKSHEET.

Source: Adapted from Estey (out of print).

Course title: _____

Lesson title: _____
[It is possible for a course to have many lessons within it; this document helps you to plan one lesson or topic at a time.]

Prerequisites: _____
[Is there anything a trainee needs to know or be able to do in order to be prepared to take this course?]

Objectives:

-
-
-

    Subobjectives: [Not every objective will include subobjectives.]

    -
    -
    -

Materials required: _____

Objective	Subobjective	Key points	How will it be taught?	Learner activities/ practice	Summary/ transition

Evaluation plan: _____
[written test, skill test, on-the-job performance]

Summary

The instructional design process might seem daunting, but it doesn't need to be. Besides it's always better to do something right the first time than it is to have to redo your work.

It is critical to conduct a needs analysis so that you are certain you are solving a training problem. Don't worry if it turns out that you don't have a training need; you have still contributed to the organization by conserving resources and identifying the actual problem. (Remember the accidental trainer's role as a performance improvement specialist mentioned in Chapter One? Identifying the real problem falls neatly into that role.) A simple design process like ADDIE will help you organize your thoughts, create a framework you can use to communicate with others, and produce a record that you can refer back to when training needs to be revised or if the training resolution did not meet the organization's expectations. When it comes to designing training, there is just one rule: do it! Although the design process may seem to be time-consuming, the time spent is easily justified by the positive return your training programs will bring to the organization.

Where Do You Go from Here?

U NTIL NOW, I'VE TALKED extensively about the many roles and responsibilities associated with a training position, including budgeting, planning, building alliances, and providing and creating training programs. Among the challenges of your role are insufficient resources, ill-defined goals, and a general lack of time to get it all done. The rewards are many, however, including an ever changing variety of assignments and the satisfaction of producing long-lasting and significant results for your organization. As you grow in this role, you'll want to take on more challenging assignments and expand the realm of performance solutions you are able to offer your organization.

I'll close *The Accidental Trainer* with a look forward to what your role may be in the future. The chapter has three sections. The first focuses on your ability to make each day enjoyable and productive. The role of an accidental trainer can be overwhelming at times, but with the right techniques, you can manage your responsibilities effectively while honing your capabilities. The

second focus of this chapter is on expanding your role and the training function to a full-fledged training department when your organization is ready.
As you become more successful, your services will be more in demand, and
this section will assist you in meeting that (exhilarating) challenge. And finally,
the chapter and *The Accidental Trainer* will wrap up with a look at where your
new skills may lead you in the future.

Making Each Day Productive and Enjoyable

I think that it is safe to say that the most effective trainers are creative, efficient, and genuinely enjoy their work. You are probably already creative and
efficient, or you wouldn't have been chosen for this job. So let's focus on ways
in which you can enjoy your work amid the pressures and expectations for
your role. Here are few tips to help you survive the day-to-day challenge of
being an accidental or part-time trainer.

Take Mental Breaks

You are probably thinking, *How can I take a break when I have so much to get
done?* I've spoken with trainers who have told me that when they are engrossed
in a project, three or more hours can fly by before they even look up from
their desk or computer screen. I suggest building breaks into your routine. In
order to be effective, you must be energized and focused, and the longer you
work, the more those two qualities will fade. Try to set one-hour time limits
for yourself, and then take a mental break. Spend five to ten minutes having
a healthy snack, walk outside to enjoy the fresh air, or simply walk around
the workplace and connect with others. These short mental breaks will reju-
venate you, reduce your frustration, and help keep your head clear so you're
able to tackle the next issue. You'll be surprised at how much more you will
accomplish when you can stay focused in this way.

Keep Your Network Fresh

Every week you'll be introduced to new people in your organization with
expertise in different areas. Capture the contact information for each one,

including their areas of expertise, their personal interests in training, and any other insights you glean from them. (If you happen to learn any personal information, such as whether the person has children, pets, or particular hobbies, make a note about these as well.) While you might not require their assistance right away, chances are you'll be faced with a challenge sometime in the future that one of these individuals can help you to address and overcome. I can't tell you how many times I've been working at a client organization and have found internal resources that my accidental trainer counterpart didn't know existed.

In order to do your job well, you'll want to make sure you are knowledgeable about all of the resources within your organization and your geographical area. When you are presented with a training challenge, you have a number of paths to follow to address it.

Keep Your Network Happy

What can you do to help your network of individuals remember you? Consider holding a reception or open house two or three times a year for your network. Invite all levels of management, your "clients" (departments), de facto trainers, subject matter experts, and anyone else who has expressed an interest in what you do. Invite your external resources as well; they will appreciate the opportunity to network informally with others in your organization. Thank anyone who has helped you in the past several months, update people on the successes you've achieved, and make a point of spending a few minutes with each person. You might even "plant" a few happy course graduates among the group of invitees. Have a suggestion box on hand for people to submit ideas and feedback. This simple networking activity will keep your work and mission fresh in your colleagues' minds and will leave them with a positive impression.

Cultivate Advocates

Spreading the word about your capabilities and successes doesn't need to be your job alone. Keep track of who is good at being a trainer or who is willing to share expertise. Be sure to share how valuable they are with as many people as possible (possibly spotlight them in a training newsletter or memo). When you say good things about them, they will certainly reciprocate by advocating the value of your work.

Keep a Kudos File

In keeping with the idea of cultivating advocates, whenever you are thanked for a job well done, ask the "thanker" to write a short note for your files. If a manager sends you an e-mail with positive results from your training or a trainee sends a testimonial, keep it. This file of kudos will pick you up when you're having a bad day, it will supply you with testimonials that will assist your ongoing marketing efforts, and it will help you to recall your advocates should you need their support in the future.

Create a Personal Support Network

The reality of every trainer—whether full time, part time or accidental—is that few people understand what you do. Find people with whom you can talk, complain, and commiserate. A great place to find others in the same position is from within the ranks of your professional organizations. Try scheduling lunches or walks after work with fellow trainers, and make the "agenda" working through training issues that you may not have enough perspective or experience to address or solve.

Ask for Help

One of the most dangerous traps that many accidental trainers fall into is the belief that they must do it all themselves. Asking for assistance from more skilled or more knowledgeable people within your organization does not mean that you are incapable or have failed. It means that you are making the organization's needs paramount, and your focus is on the best approach to your challenge. Forming an advisory committee, identifying de facto trainers, and using outside resources when you are able all contribute to a well-managed training function.

By creating an environment in which you can be successful and enjoy your work, you'll also be creating the core of a recognized training culture in your organization. Your successful implementations and problem-solving approaches will be valued and in demand. Circumstances may even start to push your organization toward expanding the training function.

Laying the Groundwork for Creating a Full-Fledged Training Department

If you are diligent and apply many of the skills you've learned in this book, you might become incredibly successful in your organization. This is the ultimate good news–bad news situation. What a wonderful achievement when an organization embraces the value of training! However, you might not be able to keep up with the demand for your services.

This will be the time to lay the groundwork for a larger training organization. It's not as difficult as it might seem. You've kept track of the people in the organization who enjoy being trainers, have helped you to develop content, or have benefited from the results of your training interventions. Start with a subtle grassroots effort. Find out who, if any, of your contacts would be interested in considering making training a full-time job. Then conduct an organization-wide survey or call a meeting of your management task force and ask them to help you develop a training plan for the next one to three years. With this information, you can create a business plan for an expanded training department that includes the resources you may need, suggestions for obtaining those resources, and a prioritized plan considering all projects for the next twelve to thirty-six months.

The business plan should also include information on how much you could continue to accomplish by yourself, how much would be accomplished with a larger team, how the team would fit into the organization, and milestones the organization could use to judge whether the expanded training department has been successful. Take it slow. Do not try to make the transition from one person to fifteen people right away. Start with small increases of one or two people, with suggestions to increase the team after major milestones have been met. A slow-growth approach will help your fledgling department to achieve success and prove its worth without becoming over-whelmed in managing itself. A first priority should be to garner administrative help, even if it is only on a part-time basis. The myriad of details that need to be addressed when creating and producing training can be a drain to your creativity and are enormously time-consuming. Knowing that a capable per-son is in charge of such matters as registering participants, ordering work-books, and following up on evaluations will enable you to take on greater and more fulfilling challenges.

If your proposal is a success, the organization will realize the benefits of a more formalized training department. High-priority projects can be rolled out more quickly because there are more training resources on hand for devel-opment and deployment. Curriculum development can become more strate-gic by appointing specialists in each business group. Internal talent can be nurtured to perform needs analysis or teach portions of a curriculum, which will enable you to reduce your dependence on outside trainers, developers, and other contractors and vendors. The processes and networks you devel-oped as an accidental trainer will become the framework on which the larger organization is built.

Where Can You Go Next?

You are actually in quite an enviable position. You may not have started your career planning to become a trainer (few of us did), but I am sure you will be thankful that you have had this opportunity.

During your tenure in training, you will have the chance to work with many departments, outside vendors, and experts from many different fields. You probably have a sense of which managers are most effective, what jobs are most difficult, and what teams have the best work environments. Who else in the organization has this type of knowledge? You will be one of the most knowl-edgeable people in your organization. In addition, you will have developed skills along the way that will enhance your career options exponentially. The box illus-trates just a few of the skills you will have developed in your role as trainer.

The Accidental Trainer Résumé

Capabilities

Organized self-starter. Can take projects from idea to completion on time and on budget. Able to work well with and through others. Proven contributions to organizational goals including monetary savings, reduced time to market, increased revenue, and workplace efficiencies.

Experience

- Performance improvement consultant
- Project management
- Event planning and production
- Marketing and promotion
- Research
- Budgeting
- Group facilitation
- Surveying
- Curriculum design and development
- Evaluation of training, including ROI
- Team building
- Leadership
- Vendor procurement and management
- Negotiation
- Networking
- Coaching and mentoring

So what now? What is the next step in your personal career development? One option is for you to embrace training and development as a career. You may decide to specialize in curriculum development, stand-up training, e-learning, evaluation, or training management. You will have had the opportunity to try all of these things, so you will know what you are most skilled at and, more important, you'll have an idea of what it is you enjoy doing. If you are thinking of making training and development your career, consider getting training for yourself. (It's a sad but true fact that trainers get less formal training in their field than do most of their clients.) At least once a quarter, consider taking a course to develop your stand-up platform skills, instructional design skills, or other skills related to your day-to-day responsibilities. Don't forget the possibility of a more formal degree program in training and development as well.

If your training department grows to include other people, you'll have the opportunity to become a training manager. To help ensure your success as a training manager, some frontline management courses might be in order. Prepare yourself for this eventuality by taking advantage of the training you are procuring for your organization. Rather than passively listening to management training courses taught by outside vendors, actively participate in them. By constantly sharpening your own skills, you'll be the model of a well-managed training department.

At some point you may decide that you want to leave the training and development function and work in another area of your organization or even in another company. You've certainly developed the project management, people management, and negotiation skills that will make you an asset to any team. You know how to prioritize, delegate, and find expedient ways to meet deadlines with the resources available to you; you are a consummate multitasker and maintain a positive, can-do attitude.

In essence, you will have worked in many of the departments of your organization. Spend time reviewing your files and take notes on what you liked and didn't like about each project. Try to imagine yourself working in that department, working in that job, or working for that manager. If you can't imagine it at all, it's probably not a position you want to pursue. If you can imagine it, set up informational interviews to renew your acquaintance with the department, and try to discover if there are any opportunities for you. Many managers would jump at the opportunity to hire someone who created the training for the job they are going to perform. After all, who knows the job better?

You may remember that in the first chapter I said being an accidental trainer can be both exhilarating and exhausting. Doing this job well will at times cause you to feel frustrated, overwhelmed, and out of control. When that happens, take a mental break and come back to reexamine your priorities. Don't hesitate to ask for help. Getting here might have been an accident, but you needn't stay an accidental trainer forever. Embrace each new day as an opportunity to learn new skills, improve your organization, and contribute to the success of your colleagues. Be creative, decisive, and focused on assisting your organization in meeting its performance goals. You are now one of the most valued assets in your organization. Congratulations!

Additional Resources

Presentation Skills and Train the Trainer

Bob Pike Group, www.bobpikegroup.com
Covers all the basics a new trainer needs to know, including presentation skills, instructional design, and adult learning methods.

Langevin Learning Services, www.langevinonline.com
Offers twenty-four workshops that cover all facets of the training function. Available as a public workshop or at your site.

The Training Clinic, www.thetrainingclinic.com
Public and private workshops and certificate programs. Offered as part of "preconference" offerings from many professional training associations as well.

Coaching

Coachville, www.coachville.com
The largest community of coaches in the world and the leader in coach-based learning. Directory of coaches.

International Coaching Federation, www.coachfederation.org
Find a coach, or learn to be a coach. Extensive training and support.

Public Seminars

American Management Association, www.amanet.org
Over 180 two- to five-day public seminars on everything from communication skills, to assertiveness skills, to leadership. It even offers a train-the-trainer workshop. If you have a big enough group, it will come to you to deliver the training and work with you to customize any topics.

Course Junction, www.coursejunction.com
A database of classes, workshops, seminars, and conferences ranging from project management to how to play the cello.

Find a Seminar, www.findaseminar.com
Find seminars by searching state, city, and topic. Also a handy venue directory should you need to schedule training off-site in a hotel or conference facility.

Fred Pryor Seminars, www.pryor.com
Fred Pryor seminars joined forces with Career Track years ago and therefore has an extensive product line of videos, audios, and CDs as well.

National Seminars Group, www.natsem.com
Offers more than twelve thousand seminars and conferences across the United States and Canada each year.

Training and Seminar Locator, www.TASL.com
A database of training course offerings that includes universities, industry

associations, media, and training companies. Allows you to search by topic and by location.

Training Registry, www.trainingregistry.com
A list of hundreds of trainers, consultants, and consulting services and thousands of training topics, workshops, and seminars covering all delivery media, including instructor led, Web-based or online courses, computer based training, and videos. Also listed are training room and training facility rentals.

Off-the-Shelf Materials

Advanced Training Source, http://www.atsmedia.com/
Videos, DVDs, and online programs for purchase or rent. Free previews. Search by topic, title, or talent (such as John Cleese or Stephen Covey).

BLR, www.hr.blr.com
Many training issues stem from HR policies and practices. BLR is the one-stop for all HR knowledge.

Business Training Media, www.businesstrainingmedia.com
Billed as a "one stop corporate training source"; also offers free newsletter, free magazines and articles.

Coastal, www.coastal.com
Broker of videos, handbooks, posters, CDs, DVDs, and other materials. Helpful sales reps will assist in choosing a product that is right for your audience and your budget. Free previews.

Entelechy, www.unlockit.com
Customizable training materials.

Enterprise Media, http://www.enterprisemedia.com
Offers training videos on customer service, sexual harassment, leadership, sales, diversity, managing change, team building, motivation, and hiring and empowering employees, as well as a variety of other management topics.

Great Circle Learning, www.trainingcontent.com
Great Circle Learning offers downloadable content. You will receive electronic source files (including the Leader Guide, slides, and participant materials) ready to use, or you can customize to the nuances of your own organization. Over thirty topics available, including managing team conflict, critical thinking, and team selling. You may also request a review copy online.

HRD Press, www.HRDPress.com
Loads of off-the-shelf training that will save you design time and have you delivering effective programs by the end of the week. Also offers assessments and resource books.

Planet Learn, www.planetlearn.com
Self-paced training for computer users and information technology professionals.

Talico, www.talico.com
Surveys, assessments, and training materials.

Training ABC. www.trainingabc.com
A huge selection of training videos.

Consultants and Contract Trainers

ASTD Buyer's Guide, www.astd.org/BG
An easy-to-use online reference for all the training sources you may need.

Chief Learning Officer, www.clomedia.com/sourcebook
This Web site for *Chief Learning Officer* magazine has an online directory listing all sorts of outsourcing options from individual trainers to large consulting firms. You'll find solutions from safety training to business writing to e-learning content and more! Fifteen minutes spent here could save you days of work.

eLance, www.elance.com
eLance provides a Web-based solution that enables small and medium-sized businesses to easily outsource projects to a global pool of high-quality service providers, including business skills, technical skills, and sales training.

ProSavvy, www.ProSavvy.com

Access to twenty thousand consultants who will bid on your project specifi-
cations. Also take advantage of ProSavvy's online resources, including templates, case studies, newsletters, and white papers.

Training Outsourcing, www.TrainingOutsourcing.com

Training Outsourcing has created an impressive list of training companies by
region of the United States. Click on Find a Training Company in the top
menu bar.

Software to Create Computer-Based Training

Camtasia, http://www.techsmith.com

Enables you to make full-motion recordings of computer-based applications,
including voice-over instructions and system audio.

Robohelp, http://www.macromedia.com/software/robohelp/

The fastest, easiest way to create professional help systems and documenta-
tion for desktop and Web-based applications.

VoxProxy, http://www.voxproxy.com

An easy-to-install plug-in for PowerPoint that adds talking, animated char-
acters to slides. Perfect for creating self-study training programs.

Miscellaneous Resources

Great Circle Learning, www.gclearning.com

GCL's *LeaderGuide Pro* is the easiest (training) manual creation tool you can
use. Create consistent and logical leaders' guides, and from them, the product automatically creates your workbooks and slides. There is no wasted effort;
everything blends together seamlessly.

Pfeiffer, www.pfeiffer.com

THE name in training and development publishing. Pick any training topic
you can think of, and you'll find a publication. And loads of free checklists
and resources are available as downloads from the site.

Trainers Warehouse, www.trainerswarehouse.com
One-stop shopping for cool tools of the training trade. This is the stuff you
can't find anywhere else: royalty-free music, flip chart stands and carry cases,
a palm-sized laptop sound amplifier, an electronic game of *Jeopardy* (just supply the questions and answers), and lots more. If you are looking for something to make your life as a trainer easier, these folks have it.

Professional Associations

American Society for Training and Development (ASTD), www.astd.org
The only U.S. and international professional society dedicated exclusively to
the needs of training professionals. Over forty thousand members nationally
and local chapters throughout the United States.

International Society for Performance Improvement (ISPI), www.ISPI.org
Dedicated to improving human performance in the workplace. National and
local chapter membership available.

Society for Human Resource Management (SHRM), www.SHRM.org
The world's largest association devoted to human resource management. Over
five hundred local chapters nationwide.

References

Bozarth, J. *e-Learning Solutions on a Shoestring: Help for the Chronically Underfunded Trainer.* San Francisco: Jossey-Bass, 2005.

Charles, C. L., and Clarke-Epstein, C. *The Instant Trainer.* New York: McGraw Hill, 1998.

Estey, H. *Five Elements of Instructional Design.* Bristol, Conn.: BVC Publishing, out of print.

Friedmann, S. *Meetings and Event Planning for Dummies.* Hoboken, N.J.: Wiley, 2003.

McCoy, C. P. *Managing a Small HRD Department: You Can Do More Than You Think.* San Francisco: Jossey-Bass, 1993.

Taylor, A. "Training Spotlight: Electrical Systems." *Maintenance Solutions,* Oct. 2004.

"2004 Industry Report." *Training Magazine,* Oct. 2004.

Wholey, J. S., Hatry, H. P., and Newcomer, K. E. *Handbook of Practical Program Evaluation* (2nd ed.). San Francisco: Jossey-Bass, 2004.

Index

About the Author

DR. NANETTE MINER is president of The Training Doctor, LLC, a firm with offices in Connecticut and South Carolina that specializes in human performance consulting, custom training design, and the delivery of training-related workshops geared to help accidental trainers.

She serves on the boards of a number of professional associations related to training and development and is a frequent speaker at industry conferences on learning, measuring business results, and leveraging limited learning and development resources for maximum business impact. She has written dozens of articles, including a regular column on training in the workplace, and has authored or coauthored a number of books. She has a doctorate in adult learning theory, a master's in training and organizational development, and a bachelor's in business and communications.

Pfeiffer Publications Guide

This guide is designed to familiarize you with the various types of Pfeiffer publications. The formats section describes the various types of products that we publish; the methodologies section describes the many different ways that content might be provided within a product. We also provide a list of the topic areas in which we publish.

FORMATS

In addition to its extensive book-publishing program, Pfeiffer offers content in an array of formats, from fieldbooks for the practitioner to complete, ready-to-use training packages that support group learning.

FIELDBOOK Designed to provide information and guidance to practitioners in the midst of action. Most fieldbooks are companions to another, sometimes earlier, work, from which its ideas are derived; the fieldbook makes practical what was theoretical in the original text. Fieldbooks can certainly be read from cover to cover. More likely, though, you'll find yourself bouncing around following a particular theme, or dipping in as the mood, and the situation, dictate.

HANDBOOK A contributed volume of work on a single topic, comprising an eclectic mix of ideas, case studies, and best practices sourced by practitioners and experts in the field.

An editor or team of editors usually is appointed to seek out contributors and to evaluate content for relevance to the topic. Think of a handbook not as a ready-to-eat meal, but as a cookbook of ingredients that enables you to create the most fitting experience for the occasion.

RESOURCE Materials designed to support group learning. They come in many forms: a complete, ready-to-use exercise (such as a game); a comprehensive resource on one topic (such as conflict management) containing a variety of methods and approaches; or a collection of like-minded activities (such as icebreakers) on multiple subjects and situations.

TRAINING PACKAGE An entire, ready-to-use learning program that focuses on a particular topic or skill. All packages comprise a guide for the facilitator/trainer and a workbook for the participants. Some packages are supported with additional media—such as video—or learning aids, instruments, or other devices to help participants understand concepts or practice and develop skills.

- *Facilitator/trainer's guide* Contains an introduction to the program, advice on how to organize and facilitate the learning event, and step-by-step instructor notes. The guide also contains copies of presentation materials—handouts, presentations, and overhead designs, for example—used in the program.

• *Participant's workbook* Contains exercises and reading materials that support the learning goal and serves as a valuable reference and support guide for participants in the weeks and months that follow the learning event. Typically, each participant will require his or her own workbook.

ELECTRONIC CD-ROMs and Web-based products transform static Pfeiffer content into dynamic, interactive experiences. Designed to take advantage of the searchability, automation, and ease-of-use that technology provides, our e-products bring convenience and immediate accessibility to your workspace.

METHODOLOGIES

CASE STUDY A presentation, in narrative form, of an actual event that has occurred inside an organization. Case studies are not prescriptive, nor are they used to prove a point; they are designed to develop critical analysis and decision-making skills. A case study has a specific time frame, specifies a sequence of events, is narrative in structure, and contains a plot structure—an issue (what should be/have been done?). Use case studies when the goal is to enable participants to apply previously learned theories to the circumstances in the case, decide what is pertinent, identify the real issues, decide what should have been done, and develop a plan of action.

ENERGIZER A short activity that develops readiness for the next session or learning event. Energizers are most commonly used after a break or lunch to stimulate or refocus the group. Many involve some form of physical activity, so they are a useful way to counter post-lunch lethargy. Other uses include transitioning from one topic to another, where "mental" distancing is important.

EXPERIENTIAL LEARNING ACTIVITY (ELA) A facilitator-led intervention that moves participants through the learning cycle from experience to application (also known as a Structured Experience). ELAs are carefully thought-out designs in which there is a definite learning purpose and intended outcome. Each step—everything that participants do during the activity—facilitates the accomplishment of the stated goal. Each ELA includes complete instructions for facilitating the intervention and a clear statement of goals, suggested group size and timing, materials required, an explanation of the process, and, where appropriate, possible variations to the activity. (For more detail on Experiential Learning Activities, see the Introduction to the *Reference Guide to Handbooks and Annuals*, 1999 edition, Pfeiffer, San Francisco.)

GAME A group activity that has the purpose of fostering team spirit and togetherness in addition to the achievement of a pre-stated goal. Usually contrived—undertaking a desert expedition, for example—this type of learning method offers an engaging means for participants to demonstrate and practice business and interpersonal skills. Games are effective for team building and personal development mainly because the goal is subordinate to the process—the means through which participants reach decisions, collaborate, communicate, and generate trust and understanding. Games often engage teams in "friendly" competition.

ICEBREAKER A (usually) short activity designed to help participants overcome initial anxiety in a training session and/or to acquaint the participants with one another. An icebreaker can be a fun activity or can be tied to specific topics or training goals. While a useful tool in itself, the icebreaker comes into its own in situations where tension or resistance exists within a group.

INSTRUMENT A device used to assess, appraise, evaluate, describe, classify, and summarize various aspects of human behavior. The term used to describe an instrument depends primarily on its format and purpose. These terms include survey, questionnaire, inventory, diagnostic, survey, and poll. Some uses of instruments include providing instrumental feedback to group members, studying here-and-now processes or functioning within a group, manipulating group composition, and evaluating outcomes of training and other interventions.

Instruments are popular in the training and HR field because, in general, more growth can occur if an individual is provided with a method for focusing specifically on his or her own behavior. Instruments also are used to obtain information that will serve as a basis for change and to assist in workforce planning efforts.

Paper-and-pencil tests still dominate the instrument landscape with a typical package comprising a facilitator's guide, which offers advice on administering the instrument and interpreting the collected data, and an initial set of instruments. Additional instruments are available separately. Pfeiffer, though, is investing heavily in e-instruments. Electronic instrumentation provides effortless distribution and, for larger groups particularly, offers advantages over paper-and-pencil tests in the time it takes to analyze data and provide feedback.

LECTURETTE A short talk that provides an explanation of a principle, model, or process that is pertinent to the participants' current learning needs. A lecturette is intended to establish a common language bond between the trainer and the participants by providing a mutual frame of reference. Use a lecturette as an introduction to a group activity or event, as an interjection during an event, or as a handout.

MODEL A graphic depiction of a system or process and the relationship among its elements. Models provide a frame of reference and something more tangible, and more easily remembered, than a verbal explanation. They also give participants something to "go on," enabling them to track their own progress as they experience the dynamics, processes, and relationships being depicted in the model.

ROLE PLAY A technique in which people assume a role in a situation/scenario: a customer service rep in an angry-customer exchange, for example. The way in which the role is approached is then discussed and feedback is offered. The role play is often repeated using a different approach and/or incorporating changes made based on feedback received. In other words, role playing is a spontaneous interaction involving realistic behavior under artificial (and safe) conditions.

SIMULATION A methodology for understanding the interrelationships among components of a system or process. Simulations differ from games in that they test or use a model that depicts or mirrors some aspect of reality in form, if not necessarily in content. Learning occurs by studying the effects of change on one or more factors of the model. Simulations are commonly used to test hypotheses about what happens in a system—often referred to as "what if?" analysis—or to examine best-case/worst-case scenarios.

THEORY A presentation of an idea from a conjectural perspective. Theories are useful because they encourage us to examine behavior and phenomena through a different lens.

TOPICS

The twin goals of providing effective and practical solutions for workforce training and organization development and meeting the educational needs of training and human resource professionals shape Pfeiffer's publishing program. Core topics include the following:

Leadership & Management

Communication & Presentation

Coaching & Mentoring

Training & Development

e-Learning

Teams & Collaboration

OD & Strategic Planning

Human Resources

Consulting

What will you find on pfeiffer.com?

- The best in workplace performance solutions for training and HR professionals

- Downloadable training tools, exercises, and content

- Web-exclusive offers

- Training tips, articles, and news

- Seamless online ordering

- Author guidelines, information on becoming a Pfeiffer Affiliate, and much more

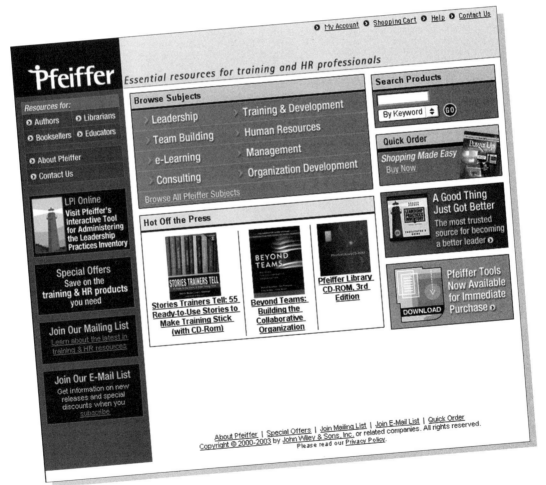

Discover more at www.pfeiffer.com